Answers

Heaven Speaks

By

Joseph P. Moris

And His Spiritually Intuitive Daughter

Marisa P. Moris

This book is dedicated to:
Jeff
Mama (aka Gleda)
Lala Chavez
Jose Chavez
Joseph Moris Sr.
Betty Moris
Joshua Moris

And our Guides and Teachers:

Our Higher Selves
Abraham
Jeremy
Eden
Delores
Alana

All of which contributed so much, both in spirit and in life!!

We are so grateful!

Intuition Publishing
1054 2nd Street
Encinitas, CA 92024

info@discoverintuition.com
www.spiritualbutnotreligious.me

Edited by Lena J. Rumps, MSEL
Formatted by Roger C. Bull
Cover design by Randy Cunningham
Interior design by Randy Cunningham

Printed in the United States of America
First Edition: August 2013

20 19 18 17 16 15 14 13 12 11 (??????)
Library of Congress Cataloging-in-Publication Data

Answers – Heaven Speaks
Joseph P Moris and Marisa P Moris

p.   cm.
ISBN 978-0-9898851-0-2

1.) Religion 2.) Spirituality 3.) Christianity (????)

Always be humble and gentle. Because of your love, be patient with each other, making allowance for each other's faults.

Make every effort to keep yourselves united in the Spirit, binding you together with peace.

There is one body and one Spirit, just as also, you have been called to one glorious hope for the future.

Ephesians 4:2-4

Table of Contents

Page

Joseph's Introduction

This book will take about two to three hours to read. It will take you away from listening to music, watching situational comedies, reality shows or just being bored and looking out the window in a car or airplane. This is a short read with some eye-popping revelations. What follows is something that my daughter and I have discovered through her phenomenal talents while working in the Light of God with His permission. My daughter can speak with the "other side". The reason why she has this ability is further explained throughout our book.

Marisa and I have spent countless hours discussing and taping what comes forward in these pages. Initially we were very confused by what "they" (to be identified shortly) were trying to teach us. I decided to transcribe the tapes, but it was laborious, and I still wasn't learning what I needed to learn. Worse yet, I was immersing myself into this as a devout Christian, too. My mind was flitting all over the place, and I was truly trying to figure out whether or not this was the right thing to do. All I could hear in my head was "Satan is the great Deceiver". The teachers from the "other side" told Marisa that I needed to just listen to the recordings while in a relaxed state of body and mind and then write the manuscript in my own words, not theirs. (I cheated a little and included various transcriptions when appropriate.)

As they explained to us, "they" knew I needed to reduce quantum physics down to simple math, so what we have brought to this book is a foundation. It is what Marisa and I have learned from teachers sent by Christ/God/Holy Spirit. "Spiritual, but not Religious" need not cringe. Just keep reading and then come to your own conclusion. And, Christians, please don't do elevator eyes yet. Please keep reading. You are not going to go to hell after reading this book.

This book is meant to bridge the gap between Christianity and Spirituality. It is meant to bring truth to both.

My brother, Randy, says that I'm trying to protect my daughter in this book. I thought about that and realized that, yes, I am protecting Marisa because she has the ability to connect with the "other side of life" in order to help people who are lost or confused. There are testimonials a little further in this book that have been written from the deepest parts of the hearts of those clients of Marisa's who have sought out her help. The "other side" told Marisa and me through her, that what they have given us is very important information for people to understand at this time of universal change. We humans don't have a clue about what is going on around us.

When Marisa and I do our Sunday sessions together, I listen to the words that flow from her. When she is channeling, she sounds like she is reading the words directly from a teleprompter, except that her eyes are closed and she only opens them when she would like to submit some input of her own. When we revisit these conversational recordings later, we notice that her voice shows a distinct difference in intonation and vocabulary.

All that follows in this little book comes from our hearts and from the direction of God. We hope the following pages will help open your mind and heart to the revelation that you probably suspect, anyway.

We had several of Marisa's clients read the drafts of this book. Marla Anthony, whose testimonial you'll read, wrote the following. I loved it:

Add something like this for example. Have you ever wondered if there are more answers than are found in the Bible? And how would you feel knowing that you had guides and angels that God put in charge of you?

Marisa and I know that the suggestions will never end because this is such a fabulous subject. Since I am a father and over time have become, by all rights, a somewhat dogmatic Christian, I think of this work now as parents and children coming together in each other's understandings of God, the cosmos, the "other side." To us, this is the chance to bridge the

Spirituality and Christianity gap, or at least allow both sides to discuss the issue better and without hard feelings.

Marisa always seeks the protection of God before ever commencing her discussions with the other side. This is a typical prayer that Marisa says before starting our taped conversations. The following is the exact prayer that Marisa said prior to our review session of this book with the other side, specifically when we were reviewing the chapter on Hell.

"Heavenly Father God, thank you for bringing us together tonight. First and foremost, I would like to thank you for your love, guidance, and wisdom and for giving us the ability to speak with you and your faithful workers on the other side. I would like to ask that anyone not claiming absolute 100 percent allegiance to Christ to leave now and not come back. You're not allowed here. Anyone or anything that is for our highest and best good will be allowed to enter into this sacred, safe, and clean place we have created tonight. Anyone or anything that can help us with this book, and is for our highest and best good, is allowed in this room tonight. Anyone who cannot help us with this book is not allowed in here. I am calling in Jeremy, Andrew, Eden, and Delores...any of our Guides and Teachers, I would like to call in Abraham, Yeshua, and any other guides that we have not spoken of that are for our highest and best good. Calling in Archangel Michael, Gabriel, Ariel and Raphael for protection, and I would like to call in our fifth-dimensional selves to see if you can help us with this book as well. I ask that Jesus Christ come into this room and surround this house with his Light and Shield and keep us protected from evil. Amen."

Marisa's Introduction

When we started this book a little over a year ago, the guides came in while I was doing a Reiki reading on my dad and told us that he would be writing a book. They said that it would help raise the vibration of the planet. They said FIRST and FOREMOST the reason for their coming in to give answers to his questions was to educate him so that he would not have to worry about what it was that I was doing now that I had become a healer, a channel, and a medium. They told him that he would be a kindergartener learning quantum physics. When chatting with him about the understanding I had (which was about a third-grade education), I realized that they (the guides) had a tough road ahead of them.

I have been told by several spiritual teachers that the nice thing about my belief system is that it comes directly from the information my guides have given me. Yes, I was raised sort of Christian, but a child always knows what their parents do and do not believe, regardless of what they are told. I knew my parents didn't really know or believe in God. I could see that my mom was against religion because she was raised super-religious and was not even allowed to play cards or she would go to Hell. So that was my take on religion.

I had friends that went to youth group and that was fun, but it was just a good reason to have a social night out during the school week. Eventually my dad didn't allow me to go to them for that exact reason. I was getting home much too late on a school night.

When I began working with my first REAL spiritual teacher, who I later partnered up with and began teaching with, he loved that I was a clear channel in regards to religious beliefs because I didn't have ANY. I had not read the Bible, I saw it as a big book of rhymes in an old language that was not understandable, and I didn't know anyone from any other religion other than a few friends who I grew up with in grade school that were Jewish, and a handful of Mormon friends.

My teacher enjoyed the fact that I could get information from the guides without throwing my intellectual, emotional, or egoic thought patterns into what my higher self and guides were sharing with me. Because of this, he encouraged me to channel about these things that I wanted answers to, so I did.

The guides began coming in with AMAZING information about all the levels of Heaven, where people go when they die, where pets go, what reincarnation is all about, what Hell is, they even started talking about all the physical layers of the earth and relative dimensions. It was mind-blowing that information like this was coming through my mouth or through the pen that I was writing with while doing automatic writing (which is a form of physical mediumship).

The information they came in with was quite clear and the messages that they portrayed were astonishing. I was hooked and needed to know more. At this point I began getting curious and looking up some of these things that they would share with me and realized that many of the concepts matched different religions throughout the world. The concepts did not match one religion only, but pretty much covered about three or four primary ones. I was BEYOND FASCINATED. This is when I started talking to my dad about the information coming in. Although by that point I was a believer in Christ Consciousness, and I understood that Jesus was a human that carried the soul of Christ and came to teach us to not only do as he did here as a human but also when we cross to the other side to strive to be like Christ as well. Even though I believed all of this, for some reason, all my dad's STRONG semi-closed-minded Christian questions would get to me, and I realized why after praying and meditating about it. It's because I was attaching his questions to an experience we had with our church. He explains the whole ordeal later in the book. Even though we had an experience with a pastor's wife that soured me to the church for a brief period of time, it never once made me bitter toward Christ. I knew that the people judging us were just scared because they did not understand. They were more willing to close their eyes and turn their backs on my poor dad and go about their lives. If anything is a true sin, then a pastor turning his back on a man who was part of his church and a personal friend for twenty-five years while his daughter was "being possessed by the devil" would be that sin.

So, anyway, back to my dad's Christian questions bugging me. I felt that this book should NOT be religious in ANY way and that it should portray these new-found teachings from the guides in that "all are one and one are all." There are no religions in spirit. They are all man made. The information that has been given to me by my higher self and guides has been given to countless other humans. We all hear it in different ways and translate it to others based on who we are, what we know and our conditioning. This is why there are so many different translations of the same thing.

The hope of the guides, my dad, and I is to publish a book that will allow people from all religions to see that we are all talking about the same thing! We are all talking about God the creator, the personality of God (Christ) and US, the spirit or child of our Higher Self and our soul who is a piece of our Oversoul and ultimately Christ/Source Energy/God. We are spirits living in human bodies. Whether religion believes the Savior has returned to earth or not, it does not matter. It is still the same core belief.

That is my hope. It is my hope to bring all this new information to the people that ask me about these topics every day in sessions. I can only do two sessions a day without wiping myself out, but I do twelve a week. Each session brings new and exciting experiences and information. The things I experience while in light trance are things that I could never have even imagined just five years ago. The things said and the education they give us is MIND BLOWING! These amazing things and the knowledge behind these bring peace to so many. To me, that is AN AMAZING GIFT and blessing all in itself!

I personally have really only lost one person that I was EXTREMELY close to when I got into this stuff, so I had no real fascination with connecting to and talking to "deceased loved ones". I was happy just knowing that the person I lost was okay. So, when people started to come to see me because their father had died and they wanted to know where he was, I was VERY hesitant, but agreed to try and help. In doing this, I have learned tons of fascinating facts about the other side. This is also what I wanted to share in a book.

When my dad sent me the draft for this book, I just slapped my forehead, and thought, "He made it religious, all that info they gave and it's about Christianity". After reading further, I warmed up to it a bit. It was not until I started to allow my Christian clients to read the book and saw the changes they experienced did I start to get excited about it.

I think our next book will go a bit deeper into all of the information about the other side, but as I have told my close family, "Who knows?" I know that my dad needed to write this book in order to understand that he is not doing anything evil by learning so much about the other side. He would like to try to convince other Christians out there who are much like how he was, lost and confused by what the church was teaching. He wants to prove to those, like himself, HOW God can hear them and how God can be a part of their lives without feeling guilt or shame for not being perfect.

My dad has so much religious dogma ground into his mind. Even when I see the excitement in his eyes because the guides are answering the age-old questions that no one else can answer, he still has hesitation. His fear is that something evil may have or will creep in to tell us lies. This is especially the case when the guides come in with something that he doesn't understand or agree with, says that the Bible is not word-for-word correct, or that something MORE than what was recorded in the Bible happened. It totally freaks him out, so dedicating this book to his comfort is VERY IMPORTANT to me. I hope it helps many others who also have the same fears. (Like the rest of my family other than my mom, brother, and dad, that is.)

I see the light bulb turn on above people's heads every day when I explain to them what the guides have shared about the structure of God, Christ, Spirit, Source, etc. It's like these people have spent their whole life wanting to be "good" and saying they were believers, but when they are told what my Higher Self said to me on Easter of 2011, (story told later in the book) it's like it all makes sense to them. The energy that I see around them almost immediately turns into relief. IT'S SO AWESOME it gives me the chills as I write this! I almost cry every time I tell the story because it was such a huge day in my life. I am told after people leave our session that they, too, have a changed life! I believe that a big part of the reason is because they now have proof that there is someone or something out there watching after them, listening to their prayers, and taking action in their lives, and that they don't have to be alone, EVER!

Marisa Moris/Daughter

Preface

I want to teach you what I have learned so far from the "other side" of life. I am a Christian, so I present this information in a way that a curious and surprised Christian would. Marisa, my daughter, who is a conduit/clear channel to the "other side," comes forward with the hope of reaching out to those who are skeptics of God—the agnostics and the atheists, as well as to other spirit-driven individuals. We hope they will find truth somewhere in here. Marisa and I wish to get through to different audiences, but truth is still the truth, no matter who it is being presented to.

I would like to explain, to the best of my ability, what has been taught to me through conversations with the other side. I ask the questions and Marisa channels the answers. The answers come from what most of us might call angels. But these angels, as we call them, have names. Some of them like to describe themselves more succinctly as healers, teachers, guides, and ascended masters (Marisa's choice). There is a hierarchy of angels, too. God has given Marisa the ability to be a spiritual intuitive and converse with the unseen. She has the ability to tap into the other side, the heavenly side, so that they can tell us what happens over there and help us to understand why we are who we are and what our purpose in life and our lessons are. Here is a transcription:

Each soul is given a guide who is with us from the birth of our soul. Others who may or may not be former humans also come in as spirit teachers. Some may stay with us a whole lifetime, while others may come and go as needed, based on the lessons an individual is learning at any given time in their life. We also have angels who stop car accidents. They are there to protect us and to be messengers taking our prayers to God.

There are questions that eventually haunt most of us. Frequently we wonder and ask questions that start with the words *why*, *what*, and *how*. Why are we who we are? What is going on around us? What awaits us when we die? What happens to good people who don't believe in God? How could God allow innocent children to be gunned down by evil when there is also so much beauty and love surrounding us as well?

There are many, many books on the subjects of near-death experiences and going through the light and meeting God on the other side. I have read a smattering of these books. I have also seen numerous television shows that have investigated such topics as angels and ghosts and UFOs along with the mysteries of places like Stonehenge, Easter Island and the many pyramids around the world. Why and what are these things here?

But the angels have asked me to make it clear that what comes forth in the following pages is truth delivered by them to us through our sessions with them. We have well over 100 hours of taped sessions. This book is about what we have learned strictly through conversing with the "other side".

Although it seems as if I have been searching all my adult life for truth, any references that I make to any books or other outside material is only a means that allows me to make requests and to submit questions to them. In no way am I validating or invalidating any of those books, authors, or other materials. That said, I recently read *Proof of Heaven* by Dr. Eben Alexander, the neurosurgeon who had a near-death experience and I also reread Pastor Bruce Wilkinson's *The Prayer of Jabez*.

Dr. Alexander writes about his first-hand experience of feeling and experiencing God's next step after he contracted a rare virus and lived in a coma for two weeks. That is how his agnostic nature as a surgeon was reversed. Dr. Alexander experienced a guide on the other side that he thought was a guardian angel.

Pastor Bruce Wilkinson is an author who encourages his readers to follow a simple prayer to God every day. By doing so, he says, you will be blessed. When his book first came out in 2001, I practiced what he preached and was awarded with a sweepstakes win in a Bank of America promotion thirty days later. I was going through a marriage separation at the time, and I used the money to settle my now former wife in a home of her own, a move that brought great peace to my adult children and to me. As you might suppose, reading Pastor Wilkinson's book and saying that prayer daily had an immediate impact on me.

The theme of these two books is that there is a loving, merciful God and that for some, God and his magnificence can be found through faith and prayer. But some men, like Dr. Alexander, have to die first to find proof of God's existence and grandeur.

Reading our book should be easier than going the route of Dr. Alexander. Being able to visualize what is going on around us is easier than you think. It doesn't require a ride through the white light to learn the mystery.

I have come to understand God in a more than religious way. Through conversations with my daughter, who has this uncanny ability, I have learned what this world is all about. The angelic teachers who have communicated with us say that trying to teach us what Heaven and God are like is like trying to teach a kindergarten child quantum physics. But as they said, it can be done! If there is a good enough explanation, even a child can understand who God is. In fact, children under six may be able to teach us what God is like better than we can teach them. Angels surround and accompany children until they hit an age of accountability, which is when a child begins to understand the difference between right and wrong. Here is what Eden said:

Eden: "Actually Joe, Angels and guides continue in every human's presence, but the sense of perception that they are there dims after the child's human ego, intellectual mind, and emotions begin to be programmed by the world around them."

That's what this little book is about: understanding who we are and why we are here. What we are learning is "Answers."

Some Answers

We have lived many lives. But we don't remember them. We, collectively, have heavenly-mandated amnesia. We don't remember starting our lives in Heaven before being born as humans. As in the Old Testament and Paul in the New Testament proclaim that God said (I am paraphrasing here), "I have known you before the filament of the earth and every hair on your head is counted" (Jeremiah 1:5 and Luke 12:7). We existed before we were born on earth. We came with personality and spirit, and we leave with personality and spirit. Our bodies, our vessels as they are called up there, remain here on earth, their usefulness completed.

Jesus also had amnesia until His baptism in the Jordan River by John the Baptist. After His baptism, Jesus began and concluded His planned mission on earth as a teacher and healer. After His baptism, He had the ability to communicate with the other side. On the other side, He was Christ, who built the universe and everything in it. On this side, He was a man who housed the soul of Christ. He no longer prayed to the Father in blind faith, for after His baptism, His angelic guides lifted the amnesia from His human mind and ego. His ministry commenced and then He died on a cross and was resurrected to rejoin His collective consciousness, His Higher Self (Lord), which was none other than Christ, who is the Personality of God living with the first soul, the Holy Spirit within.

The prophets of old who preceded Him laid down the signs of Jesus' (Yeshua's) coming in many places in the Old Testament, with most of the signs in the books of Isaiah, Jeremiah, and Daniel which in today's terms are channeled books with all the visitations from the "Lord". Christ had visited earth many times before becoming Jesus, the man, and He will come again. He was Krishna several thousand years earlier, and He was also Melchizedek who met Abraham (Abram). Abraham was the founder of the Hebrew faith about 2,000 years before His coming as Yeshua, or Jesus Christ.

18

We come from our true home in Heaven. As odd as this may sound, Heaven is reality and earth is basically a Petrie dish where a duality of good and evil is allowed to co-exist. A planet with the duality of good and evil co-existing in the universe is rare, so despite the relatively young age of earth (their words); our collective consciousness leads us to believe that we are the center of the universe. Here is what they said about that:

Higher Self: There are many other realms, many other universes, many other dimensions and many other earths, some of which may not even know about our earth. Technically Joe, we do not agree that this earth is the center of the universe, but as a figure of speech, yes, there are many spiritual visitors who are watching and guiding us in order to help the earth become more like their planets. Because of this activity, our earth feels like it's the center of the universe. These visitors have watched as baby planets, like earth, developed and learned to sustain all forms of life, including humans. Unfortunately, they have watched these humanoids destroy their planets completely, so they need to recreate a new planet, like earth with animal life, plant life, oceans, rivers, and streams so that humans may be developed to the point, as in the planets that surround the Pleiades, Arcturus, Andromeda, and Sirius, to evolve so that souls will be willing to incarnate into these humanoids. With the earth's duality, their souls like to incarnate on earth for the experience. Currently, even today in 2013, twenty percent of the earth's humans are souls that have lived on other planets.

From the true home of everyone who has lived and died on earth, selected angels are watching this grand experiment that you and I are here to endure by design. We designed our lives in Heaven with the help of our spirit guides and the approval of our Souls. We also come from a Spiritual family in Heaven, a family that continues to incarnate together over time on earth in order to learn the lessons that our Souls predetermine us to experience. These are our soul mates, our soul family and soul group.

The only huge caveat is that *we are born with amnesia by design*. We don't remember where we came from. We are spirit and we have lived before.

Prologue

We live in a very strange time. Life is fast. Nothing is slow anymore…except maybe baseball.

I fondly remember the 80s, more specifically, the early to mid-80s. Cell phones and computers had not yet found their way into our lives. My kids were growing up and it was fun being a part of their growing. When the workday was done, it was usually finished. It was home to the family and tending to family business. Spirituality was not a big deal although each day as I drove the kids to school we would say the Lord's Prayer and then follow with another prayer that I made up. It went like this:

Thank you, God, for another day. Thank you for taking care of me and my family. Bless me in all that I do and keep me holy. In Jesus' name, Amen.

It was a simple prayer, a small attempt to connect with God. I was brought up in a Christian Science home. My dad was Baptist, but he wasn't into religion at all. My mom studied her copy of Mary Baker Eddy's *Science and Health with Keys to the Scriptures* along with the Bible. She had lots of tabs in both books. It wasn't until I was about fourteen that on Sundays my parents would drop my three brothers and me off at Sunday school, go have a Danish and coffee at a local diner, and then come back to church and pick us up. We would usually go home and do a bunch of work around the house. In rare cases, following church, our parents would give us a quarter and drop us off at the movies (that's what they cost in those days). And with the quarter I kept, instead of putting it into the tithing basket, I could also get popcorn and a drink. My parents seldom asked what we were taught, and if they did ask, I couldn't recall it. I only remember dreading it when it was going to be my turn to read from the Bible in front of the other kids. I didn't remember much of anything except the Lord's Prayer and some of the Ten Commandments.

My parents eventually gave up on that routine and decided to just stay home on Sundays. Out of respect for the church-goers in the neighborhood, however, we weren't allowed to go outside to play until noon. Occasionally, my mom would say something about God, but it went in one ear and out the other. God usually came up when she was mad at us, which was often. She had four boys.

That was my spiritual upbringing. I don't remember wondering who God was until I was in college, and mostly I didn't care. I had friends who had parents, usually the mother, who went to Mass almost every day. I respected that, but didn't give God any thought, much less any understanding.

While I was in college, which followed time in the army after high school, I took a religion class to fulfill a humanities requirement. I chose a class called Black Religion in America. I don't really remember learning anything in particular about the course, even though I scored an A. Strangely enough, at that time I came across a book written by Immanuel Velikovsky, the author of three controversial books written in the 1950s. He was tagged as a heretic then and only recently has come to be considered a genius decades ahead of his time. He was also a close friend with Albert Einstein. *Worlds in Collision* was his first book, in which he wrote that Venus had once been a moon of Jupiter that was thrown out of its orbit by a comet. This was in the days of the *Iliad* and the Trojan War; strangely enough, the Book of Exodus, which tells how Moses led the Hebrew tribes out of Egypt about the same time. Velikovsky created his theories through reading religious writings around the world and finding similarities in their customs and traditions.

In his second book, *Earth in Upheaval,* Velikovsky uses scientific example to show that Venus made a close pass to the Earth. The effect was to spin the earth and tip it over, reversing the axis and making the North Pole the South Pole and vice versa. In one part of the world, the sun stood still for three days. That was told in Asian and Polynesian lore…and then there was Joshua in the Old Testament standing with his army before the walls of Jericho. "And the sun stood still, and the moon stayed, until the people had avenged themselves upon their enemies" (Joshua 10:13). Velikovsky went to great scientific lengths to prove the reversed polarity in magnetized rocks around the world. Even more bizarre was his theory that the Himalayas are a relatively recent phenomenon of two geological plates smashing into each other at the sudden flip of the earth.

His findings were magnificent, but the religious aspect seemed to get to me. I proceeded from there to have some grinding thoughts about religion. I was thinking that religion must be some kind of banal cult thing with something as physical as a planet whizzing by and then linking that to the so-called gods or a one true god. It was a bit intriguing.

I actually broke down and decided to read the Bible as a historical document unfettered by any religious ideology. I found it interesting, especially Genesis. I was finding that the Old Testament, after the Exodus, was mostly boring until I got to the books of the prophets, which I remember reading with raised eyebrows. You see, the prophets are better than major rock stars. They've been memorialized for more than 3,000 years. Think about it, these men and women of old were persecuted by the religious leaders of their time. These would be the Jews, of course, after the Exodus and the claiming of their land in what is now Palestine and Israel. Prophets were portrayed as crazy. Prophets like Isaiah, Daniel, Joel, Elijah, and others were all visited by the Lord and told to foretell the future. These human souls ended up being persecuted as outcasts by their leaders, the Jews, only to have another prophet come along and be persecuted again and then be immortalized, only to be followed again by another prophet who was persecuted then immortalized. The Jews did this right up to the persecution and death of Jesus. Unfortunately, the Jewish religion still won't recognize Jesus for who He really was.

I realized that the Old Testament was a set-up for the arrival of a messiah. So when I got to the New Testament and read about the miracles of Jesus, I thought that our own science was coming close to doing some of the things He did. In other cases, like raising the dead, I wasn't quite sure how He was getting away with that. Now, like Dr. Alexander in his book, medicine and technology have been able to basically bring back the dead. I remained skeptical about God. I was a true agnostic. I never really thought of myself as an atheist, but I sure had my doubts about God. After all, the Bible says that God lives in all of us. I didn't know scientifically how that could happen, and if it did, what was that all about, anyway? What is He doing in my life? And if He does have residence in me, how come there is always some problem or crisis I am in the middle of that he can't fix? I remember my dad passing away at a young seventy-one in 1989. I told everyone he was in a better place, but all I could think of was clouds and harps. I had absolutely no concept of Heaven.

At the behest of my wife, Gleda, my family had started going to church in the early 90s as long as church didn't interfere with the kids' sports. We decided early on that for good reason, the kids should have some exposure to religion. My parents had tried with me at an impressionable age, so I thought I would at least expose my kids to God, too. But this time my wife and I also attended the church service while the kids were in Sunday school class with their peers. We liked the church we went to because they played electric guitars, the pastor and his family was young, and there was free doughnuts and coffee after the service. It was pretty cool. Sitting through the sermons was okay, but there wasn't a whole lot of convincing on my part going on. I still couldn't figure out how God was listening to everyone at the same time. That was beyond my comprehension. Besides, I kept having a hard time praying to a man named Jesus.

Then, in 1997, I heard about *The Urantia Book*. I was watching a late-night television show that usually focused on the search for extraterrestrials. I was really into that. My son and I witnessed a UFO together in 1988. I had a feeling that there was something greater than us out there and thought they had to be in spaceships, and my son Joshua and I did see something that was unexplainable. The TV show was *Strange Universe*. Oddly enough, one night they had a twenty minute segment on *The Urantia Book*. I had never heard of it before. The narrator said that every president since Eisenhower had read it and that they referred to it as the "Blue Book." Well, I had heard that the Blue Book supposedly held the secrets the government was keeping from us about UFOs. The TV show kept talking about God and making references to "guides" and "angels." I was a bit fascinated. The show closed with the words: *If you want to know the real truth about what happened in the Garden of Eden, then you should read this book.*

That definitely piqued my interest.

I found the book through an 800 information number. When I eventually received it, I opened it to the foreword and began reading. I felt like I was reading Latin. Nothing made sense. It seemed totally incomprehensible. I was having some real doubts about this book, especially its length. Nonetheless, my curiosity got me to flip to the first page of Chapter 1. The opening line went something like this: *God is your eternal Father.* I was disappointed. Though this was just a religious book, I wanted to know about UFOs, so I started reading this 2,194 page tome with its tiny type anyway. I really didn't have anything else to do after the kids went to bed other than watch television. Like any good book, it was hard to put down.

For the next three months, I was deep into reading this book about the history of the earth over the last one million years. Urantia is supposedly the celestial name for our planet. The book was mind boggling and in most cases hard to understand. It described God and how big His administration is, what it takes to run the universes, and how He eventually designed planets to evolve to the point of having human bodies capable of having spirit in them. Most of my interest though focused on the last 700 pages, the fourth section of the book. It was the life of Jesus, who was also Christ where Christ was the Personality and embodiment part of God. It was the life of Jesus for every year of His life. The first three sections of the book spoke of how God sent His agents to help the earth evolve with their tinkering. The last section just blew me away because it made a case for God as man on this earth who was assisted by members of other created levels of beings who were not ever human but were angels.

After completing *The Urantia Book*, I turned to page 1 and read it again. After that, I decided I would take another look at the Bible while also keeping the writings of Velikovsky and *The Urantia Book* in mind. What amazed me was that the Bible was now making sense. I could read a passage and sort of see it like some kind of code that needed to be used to get through to mankind in that era, but, oddly enough, for this era, too. I was coming to the belief that the Bible was the story for the masses and that Velikovsky and *The Urantia Book* were explanations for those seeking further truth. I was hooked. I came to the conclusion there was a God, but I still couldn't understand how and why He took up residence in every person, and if so, why there was good in the world but yet so much evil, too? What kind of a God is and was this that let such duality to exist together? For a Mother Teresa, there was a Hitler. That was nuts. There was a yin and a yang, a sowing and a reaping.

In 1998 I took the plunge, literally. I was baptized along with my daughter Marisa on her twenty-first birthday. I felt my whole psyche change. I couldn't explain it, but it was as if a big cloud was lifted from my shoulders and my eyes. There wasn't a booming voice welcoming me into the Kingdom of Heaven as His son, just cold water in the San Diego Harbor on a June afternoon. My daughter felt nothing. We had been baptized because she was living in a court mandated Christian rehab home for those with drug habits, and we thought it was the right thing to do.

This leads me to Marisa.

Marisa's Story
Part 1

I always thought I was a normal girl growing up in a small beach town in Southern California. For the most part I got all As, I was good at sports, and had a pack of friends that I would spend most of my time with going to movies, the mall, the beach, talking about boys and having sleepovers. Looking in from the outside, I was as normal as they came, but something inside always made me feel different, like I didn't fit in.

When I graduated from high school my best friend and I chose UCSB as our college. We had applied to eight of them in California, got accepted to them all, but I chose this one because Santa Barbara is where I was born and it was where my dad had a couple of his degrees. My friend chose it as well for reasons I can't remember. We had a dorm room all set up and waiting for us to move in. Two weeks prior to moving, I decided that because I was madly in love with my "future husband" that I was going to stay behind so we could be together. My parents were shocked, but didn't put up a fight, they just said, "Okay you are an adult, you make your own decisions."

Things got VERY strange at our house because my aunt, her drug addict husband, and their three kids had to move into our home temporarily after losing their house to foreclosure. At this time, I began to see my dad as a person, not just a dad, and I could sense how unhappy he was. We had NO communication skills back then so instead of talking to him or my mom about it, I stayed away as much as possible.

I was working full-time and taking 21 units at the local junior college so I had no time for friends, my social life was non-existent, but I was okay with it because "I was in love" (rolling my eyes) and spent every free moment with my boyfriend. One day when I was at work, my co-worker told me about how she was planning to move to Mammoth Lakes, CA to work for the mountain's resort. She said she would get to snow board for free and she was registering for school. She said it was cheap up there and the mountain's starting pay was 4 dollars more an hour than what we were making.

This sounded like HEAVEN so I talked my boyfriend into quitting the job he had at his dad's company so that we could move up there together. We moved December 15, 1995. I still remember driving away in my maroon Mercedes that was packed to the rim with things. As I watched my house get smaller and smaller out the rear view mirror. I remember thinking "I am FREE! Look out world! Here I come!"

Unfortunately my new found freedom was not what I thought it would be. The huge house I lived in was always packed with people partying, drinking, and smoking pot. It was almost impossible to get my homework done and even harder to go to sleep at night. After a month I decided to join in with all the others. I started experimenting with drugs and found myself drinking every single night. It made me nervous that I enjoyed being under the influence so much but, it didn't stop me from continuing on. Finally my boyfriend said something to me about it and we made a joint decision that it would be best to move home and get out of the unhealthy environment.

We moved home to a different town. All of my friends were gone to college. I was so jealous. I felt like a loser going to junior college and working part time. As we all know, if we feel a certain way about ourselves then this is what we become. With my new self-labeled loser identity I dropped out of school, started partying, experimenting with street drugs, and staying out nights at a time. My parents didn't know what was going on with me, but as I said before, my family's communications skills were non-existent so we just all avoided the obvious and each other.

Three months later, the boyfriend who I changed my life path for told me that he cheated on me. I told him that I didn't care, that I forgave him, and that we needed to stay together because I loved him. He told me that he felt so guilty that he couldn't even be around me. I still remember feeling like I had gotten punched in the stomach, I couldn't breathe and my life literally flashed in front of my eyes. This is the day that severe depression began to take its course in my life.

My mom finally got worried enough to take me to a doctor who gave me anti-depressants and pills to sleep at night. They made me feel better, but again, just like I had experienced in Mammoth, I started to enjoy living in an altered state more than not. I couldn't just take one pill as prescribed; I would take two, or three or even five at a time. I was on a path of self-destruction while trying to convince myself that I was happier than I had ever been. Realistically, I hated my life and I despised myself. My parents saw me as a different person and after spending a lifetime over achieving to make them proud, I was so ashamed.

Around this time I reunited with a boy I dated in high school and we began spending all of our time together. He was your stereotypical "bad boy" and that is what he was known for in our small town. I knew that he was truly a genuine, funny, lighthearted person underneath the anger, insecurity, fear and false image he felt the need to portray. These qualities are what kept me hanging on to him through thick and thin. This story is not about him so let's just put it this way; I spent the next six years of my life being a co-dependent, enabling him in his addictions, and working full-time to give him money. I took the blame for him when he got caught with drugs in my car and I eventually made the decision on my own to get hooked on drugs as well. Because of the charge I took for him, I was put in a rehabilitation program for 28 days, but I chose to stay in a Christian Recovery home for about a year after graduating. I could see that by living there my parents were not worried because it kept me away from the "bad boy". While I was living in the recovery home my dad and I were baptized together. The baptism didn't do anything for me because I didn't understand. I just felt so good seeing my dad proud of me again; it had been so long.

Now, let's fast-forward five years. By then I had cleaned up my life, messed up, cleaned up, REALLY messed up and then cleaned up for good. I had become a very successful loan officer, so much so, that my dad and I opened our own brokerage in a 2000 square foot office overlooking Moonlight Beach in Encinitas. My life was PERFECT!

In August 2007, I got the call I always feared in the prior years when I was chasing my ex-boyfriend around town, trying to save and fix him. We had not spoken in years so when I saw his mom's number pop up on my called ID, I was shocked. The call was to let me know that he had passed away because of some pharmaceuticals he took. I remember standing in the middle of my huge office, dropping the phone, getting dizzy, then flying down onto the ground into a fetal position while screaming, crying, and asking God (if there was one) "WHY?!?!"

I wanted to know where he went! I had never experienced losing someone that I loved as deeply as I thought I loved him. I started asking an invisible God that I didn't believe in for signs that my ex-boyfriend was in Heaven. I NEEDED to know he was okay! Signs would show up regularly and I would quickly dismiss them as coincidences. I was unable to concentrate on work; all I could get myself to do every day was look at old pictures and search for proof that there was something BETTER beyond the physical. I hit so many dead ends when it came to finding answers to my questions that I finally just gave up in frustration. I was completely unfulfilled so I very quickly slipped back into a depressed state, but this time I was suicidal because I had convinced myself that, had I still been helping him, he would be alive. This went on for months until my mom finally stepped in and told me to go to the psychiatrist.

The doctor told me I had Bi-Polar Disorder, ADHD, and Chronic depression. (Which coincidentally is what most of my students think they have until they learn they are also healers and/or mediums. I will explain more about that later). My new doctor wrote me a prescription for three different medications and they VERY quickly got me back on track. The only problem, and it was a huge one, was that the mediations triggered me to have seizures. The doctors did scans and all sorts of tests and came to the conclusion that for my entire life, since I was young, I had a low seizure threshold but, not until this point, had I done anything to cause my brain to go over it. They told me I was epileptic and prescribed me an anti-seizure medication to take in addition to the other meds.

The medication kept me from having seizures, and other than the fact that the medication made me gain a ton of weight; I was feeling great all around. I had started to get into reading "spiritual" books, mostly about the Law of Attraction because they taught how to make more money through simply thinking about it. It seemed to work, I was making great money, so I poked around some more with spiritual books. As if out of nowhere, co-workers and clients gave me books to read and I

31

actually read all of them from front to back. They answered so many questions about why we, as humans, do what we do and gave simple remedies for problems we had in our life or with our personality. Things were looking up. Even though I was heavier than I wanted to be, I was on a road to self-help, making great money, working around the clock, and running a marketing company in addition to being a managing partner at our office. I felt good!

Proof of my self-destructive behavior came loud and clear in May of 2008 when I made a ridiculous decision to see what would happen if I stopped taking my seizure medication. I wanted to see how much weight I could lose in a month because I was now 35 pounds heavier than I had ever been. This leads me now to the accident that changed my life.

Marisa's Story (Part 2)
Who was THAT? Who AM I!?

I had just bought a brand new Mercedes and was coming home from the mall. I was in a rush because I was late meeting my dad for church. I got off the freeway, made the left turn, and began heading toward the hill that would take me home.

The next thing I saw was completely unbelievable. I was standing above an accident scene with a girl who looked like me only she was about two feet taller, had green eyes, and blonde hair. On my left was a huge ball of light. In frustration, as if I had known them forever, I began talking to them. I told them, "There is NO way I am going back you guys, Marisa is an idiot! Look at her! She has crashed her car, she's going to lose her license, the housing market is crashing and she has no clue how broke and unhappy she is about to be! I am NOT doing it anymore and you can't make me!"

The tall girl just looked at me and with true unconditional love in her eyes, she laid her hand on my right shoulder and INSTANTLY I felt the most indescribable feeling I had ever felt. I was light; I was all knowing; I knew who I was and why I was here; my physical body didn't hurt; I felt like a four year old again! She said, "You HAVE to go back, there are too many people to help." My response to that was, "Help people do what, lose their homes? No thank you." I began to walk away still feeling like I had never felt before; I still can't describe it to this day, but it was heavenly to say the least.

Next thing I know, I wake up soaking wet with ambulance workers and police men surrounding me. I had blacked-out, had a seizure, hit a fire hydrant, and supposedly almost drowned in my own car.

My life following the accident was a living HELL. I thought I had hit bottom in the years past when I battled with drugs, this was not even close and it was horrible! I couldn't remember anything for longer than a day or two so my business began suffering. I was now living with my dad, stripped of my driver's license, and therefore, my independence. I needed to be with someone 24 hours a day just in case I had another episode. Over the next few months I had several seizures, usually one every two weeks; sometimes they spaced out three weeks if I was lucky. Although I never saw the girl that looked like me when I had those seizures, I would still regain that feeling I had when I was out of my body that night. It was the feeling of not being tied to this earth, of knowing who I was, where I was going, and what my purpose was. When I was out of my body, I didn't hurt. The feeling was true bliss. After what seemed to be a lifetime, I would abruptly come right back to my body where I would be told that I had only been unconscious for a few minutes. I felt nothing but pain and sadness; I didn't want to be in my body; I wanted to leave again!

Nine months later, I managed to get my license back. I made an agreement with the DMV and my Neurologist to submit to blood level tests once a month to make sure I was taking my anti-seizure drugs. I FINALLY felt free, I was becoming "normal", and I felt a sense of accomplishment for taking all my medications and being seizure free for such an extended amount of time.

January of 2009, One month after I started driving again, it happened AGAIN! While driving my dad's favorite car (it was like his child), I had an episode and crashed his car. This time was not as dramatic; there was no water; I was not injured; I didn't hit my head; and there were no airbags deployed, and no concussion.   Butagain, I found myself back up above the accident with the two beings I had met at my last car accident.

Needless to say, I was angry with them. I scolded them for making me go back. I told them that they had not even said goodbye when they sent me back and even worse they had not been in touch since. They said, "We have been with you the whole time, you just can't hear us through Marisa's mind." This triggered my anger even more, I yelled at them about how frustrating Marisa was. I told them, "I can't handle it, not only does she not hear you, she won't listen to me at all!" The tall girl just smiled at me again, placed her hand on my right shoulder and, BAM, I woke up in the local emergency room with my dad next to me, scared out of his mind. Shortly after, they released me to him. The car ride was so uncomfortable; we were silent the whole way home. I could feel his disappointment, anger, and sadness.

After this seizure, I was coherent enough to think that it would be a good idea to write down what happened so I could remember it. My memory was not completely back yet after losing it in the first accident, so I had gotten in the habit of writing everything down so as to not forget. In the comfort of my home, I grabbed some paper and a pen and began writing. I wrote about what had just happened when I had the seizure in my dad's car. I also wrote about what had happened the year before when I crashed my Mercedes. I scribbled out on paper the people I saw at the accident scenes, what they were wearing, the way the accident scene looked, and of course, about the conversation I had with the two mysterious beings. About a month down the road, I requested the police reports and what I found was truly astonishing! The people I had seen at the accidents were described in the police report as wearing EXACTLY what I had written down! I knew with-out a fraction of a doubt, that there was NO way I could have seen those people in the second accident because I was unconscious. My skeptical mind would wonder if I really had seen the first accident for a brief moment but had no conscious memory of it. I thought there was a chance that the information was stored in the subconscious mind and that is the primary reason that I had not given much thought to the conversation with the two mystery beings. The second accident was horrible and caused so much pain in my life and my family's, but it gave me proof that what I had seen the first time was real.

This prompted me to start a mission that would change my life and who I was forever! My newfound quest was to figure out who those two were, why they made me come back, how I could feel the way I did when I was out of my body without having a seizure, and most importantly, I wanted to know who the heck I was! If I was NOT Marisa, who was I? It was fascinating, mysterious, exciting, and extremely confusing all at the same time.

License-less again, I was going to learn to get out of my body so that I could go ask that girl, who looked like me, why she made me come back and I wanted to know who she was. I was also determined to get her to tell me who I was. I had no clue where to begin to find my answers and quickly found that there was such a lack of information about what had happened to me. Around this time in 2009, most of my memory returned, but it did not cause good things to happen in my life. I began to remember all the horrible things I had done, how I had scared and hurt my family and those that loved me. I started to see where my life had gone over the last year, and I saw where it was headed. I got VERY depressed. Every day at the office, I spent hours being annoyed, upset, frustrated, angry, and bitter at myself and expressed it in an outward fashion, projecting all of my behaviors onto the agents at the office. I took most of this out on my dad, who was constantly there with me. One day, he had enough and basically told me via email to get out of his life. He told me to go fly a kite (but not in those nice words). He said if I wanted a father to find him in Heaven.

I took his statement, as he wanted me to go kill myself so the suicidal obsession came back. It was on my mind day-in and day-out sitting in my apartment alone with nothing to do. I could not go to the office because, one, I couldn't drive, and two, my dad and I were not speaking anymore and he was my business partner. I had saved up a good amount of money from the years past; therefore, I was not worried about finances. Oddly enough this was what made me even more depressed. I didn't understand it at the time, but with what I know now, looking back, I see the reason. I was torn and depressed because ever since I had "cleaned up" five years prior my identity was based on my career and my ability to make great money. I was proud of that and I thought my family was too.

By this time, I had met and was living with the most amazing boyfriend I could have ever imagined. He was supportive, strong, logical, level headed and responsible, and he was out of town for several months leaving me home alone. When he called me daily, so as to not worry him, I would tell him everything was great! He would always have something to say that would cheer me up instantaneously; I missed him so much. At that time, waiting for him to come home was my only reason for staying alive.

One day, while I was at the drugstore across the street from our complex, a cashier that was always chatty with me handed me a CD with *The Power of Now* and *The Secret* on it. He recommended I listen to both. I thought it was nice of him, said thank you, then went home and threw it in a drawer. A couple weeks later, I had a random person mention both those books to me in a conversation at the grocery store, so I went home, got the CD out, and listened to *The Power of Now*, since it was first on the CD. I still have never gotten to *The Secret*.

The Power of Now made so much sense to me and inspired me to learn more about this so-called devious and evil ego that was HIDING in my mind. In my frame of mind at that time, I loved that by learning about the ego and how it is separate from WHO WE REALLY ARE, that I could take that knowledge and use it to blame everything bad that I had ever done and that ever happened to me on it!! "Oh," I could tell myself, "THAT wasn't ME.... THAT was my EGO!" Looking back, I laugh, but that is really what I thought at the time! What's funny is I see a good part of my students go through the same process and it makes me smile to see them grow. I obviously know now that the ego is NOT evil or devious and that it has a purpose. But at that point in my life, at the conscious level I was living at, having something other than myself to blame for all these things I was suicidal over was just what I needed to get me out of that funk.

When I overcame my suicidal tendencies and was finally getting out of the depression, I was still working very little and living on what I had left of my savings from 2007 and 2008. I dove into tons of books about human nature and why we do the things we do. I have ALWAYS been interested in this subject. I have studied Chinese astrology since I was a teen, not so much to tell the future, but to learn to categorize different personality types, their mannerisms, and each sign's probability of doing certain things and getting along with other people. I studied psychology during my short two-year stint in college and absolutely loved learning about the subconscious mind.

I started seeing all of these things to be true that I was learning in these new books I was reading. I felt driven to learn more. I loved all the knowledge I was attaining about the ego and the subconscious mind because I was able to recognize these things in people around me. Although I didn't know I had the abilities that I have now, I have ALWAYS enjoyed reading people, and this new knowledge gave me even more ammo in addition to the psychology and the Chinese astrology. I would sit for hours and hours reading websites, watching YouTube videos, and downloading audio books about this topic. Like I just said, I was not working much and I was still not driving due to the fact that the DMV needed to see a one-year "seizure free" period documented by a neurologist. I could not show them that. So, basically, I didn't really have much else to do. In essence, I was just existing and with no real life. It was sad, but I filled my time with 24/7 studying. Looking back, now I see how much of a blessing that time I had really was. My foundation was being built for what I would be doing in the future.

Once I started to believe that I was an "expert" (yeah, right!) on the topics I was studying about human behavior, the ego, the emotions, etc., I would sit on the computer and send out these quotes that I was learning from the books to others. I suppose I was hoping to inspire them to change. (Because I was perfect?) I would think, *Oh. My. Gosh! This is perfect for my sister! She NEEDS to read this!* Or *OMG, this is SOOOO perfect for my mom; I NEED to send this to her right NOW!* Or, *WOW! My dad REALLY needs to read this because it will CHANGE his life!!*

Throughout each day, as I would come across new information, I would send quotes, links, and videos out to my family members including my dad, who was no longer talking to me. I heard back from him once, and it wasn't very pretty, so I never sent another one to him. At this time, I felt it was necessary to INSPIRE all those around me by pointing out all their HORRIBLE QUALITIES so as to FIX them and make them good people. (Like I had become???)

I had not learned yet that we only see in OTHERS what we have in OURSELVES. I still remember that the first time I read about this concept, I quickly dismissed it. I thought: *There is NO WAY I am as annoying as all those people around me!*

After coming across this teaching a few more times and giving a bit more thought, I realized it was true! I have to admit it—it was a hard pill to swallow at first. In fact, I decided to prove the theory WRONG. I went back into the old emails that my dad had sent me accusing me of things that he swore I was thinking or doing, and I realized, *OMG, he is totally talking to himself!!!* The same thing happened with emails from my sister! We were not speaking at the time, either. I immediately took the immature route. I started to believe that I was SUCH a victim. I started thinking, "How dare they do this to me, they have accused me of all THEIR WRONGS!" Suddenly, and I remember this moment, something came over me and knocked me right up-side the head. (Now I am sure it was my guides.) I decided to look back at all the BRILLIANT and FABULOUS emails that I had written to my family members to see what I had accused them of. To my utter amazement, I realized that I was literally talking to myself in a mirror every time I sent those emails out! I was shocked to say the very least! I really believe that day, sitting in front of my computer and coming to that realization was the first day of the rest of my life!

From that day forward, I began to acknowledge all these things that I had become. At first, I went right back into my funk of suicidal thoughts and depression. I would think: *Why am I even here? What is my purpose for being alive since I have caused SO much pain?* I suddenly saw that EVERYTHING was MY fault and not the others around me that I had been blaming the whole time. (Again, the conscious level I was operating at believed that. I know now that this is not completely true.)

At this new low point of my life, I came across a book by Jerry and Esther Hicks called *The Power of Deliberate Intent*. I began reading it because I hoped it would help me to get out of this hopeless mental state I thought I had escaped and cured myself of but was trapped in again. The book gave simple exercises that can change your mood from sad to mad and jealous to appreciative, etc. It explained that being mad was much easier for us as humans to be than sad. That made so much sense to me. I kept reading the book and trying the exercises because at that point I was willing to do anything to not be SO SAD anymore.

Reading that book, I started to learn about the Law of Attraction and began seeing things that I wanted manifesting in my life VERY quickly. Things started getting better. I was working again, making money, and I was working on getting my driver's license back (with medical restrictions, of course). All of this happened in such a short amount of time while I was reading the book (and a few others about Law of Attraction). I absolutely fell in love with the authors and became a huge fan. I went out and bought all their books and the audio versions, too. I was constantly listening to them at work, and when I was not working I was reading. I loved how simple they made life sound, and I loved that they taught that we are the makers of our own lives. No one else is...just us! I liked that they said this because at that point myself was all I had. I had no trust in anything outside of me, including God.

One day I went online to look up these authors to see where they went to school. I was wondering how the heck they got so darn smart. How did they know all this AMAZING stuff?? I discovered that Esther Hicks was what was called a

41

"channeler," and Jerry was her husband who helped write the books. A CHANNELER?? *What the heck is a channeler??,* was my exact thought. I had no clue what one was, so I looked it up. I found that there are certain people that can channel beings that no one else can see, and that TOTALLY intrigued me. Actually, "intrigue" is not a big enough word to explain the draw and fascination I had toward this ability! Looking back, I don't know how I didn't think it was odd that I was becoming completely obsessed with channeling and channelers. I began looking for books that were channeled, and one day in the New Age section of Barnes & Noble, I ran across a book called *Opening to Channel.* I immediately thought, *OMG—I can LEARN TO CHANNEL!!! I am going to DO THIS!! YIPEEEE!*

Although I was beside myself with excitement I did not buy the book that day for one reason: I was embarrassed. Because of my upbringing and things I was taught at church, I had come to believe that all the books in the New Age section were of the devil. It's funny to look back now at how I would go about reading books from that section. What I would do, was I would set up camp over by the Christian section, which was right next to the New Age-astrology section. I figured if anyone saw me, I would be there and they wouldn't think anything of it. I figured if they saw what I was reading, I could say that I found it in the astrology section, knowing that astrology is accepted by most Christians and is not thought to be evil. I felt good about this setup I had designed. Every ten minutes or so, if no one was around, I would slowly and casually walk through the New Age section. I would quickly grab a few books of interest, then scurry back to my station near the Christian books where I had set up camp. I laugh so hard at myself now, but I know now that it was all part of my growth, and it also helps me relate to others like me going through the same things in their lives. I didn't buy the book about channeling out of fear that someone would see me with it, but went straight home to order it on Amazon. Along with it, I bought another recommended book by the same author. It was called *Becoming Your Higher Self*. I placed the order for next day delivery and eagerly awaited the knock at my door from UPS.

At that time Jeff, my boyfriend, knew NOTHING about the things I had begun to learn. I am glad because had I told him (or anyone else, for that matter), he or they would have told me I was nuts (just as I would have said to myself six months earlier). If that had happened, I probably would have just dropped everything and I would not be where I am today.

Luckily for me and my secret studies, Jeff was working a lot and left at least four nights a week and stayed at hotels, leaving me home alone. I took full advantage of this time to read my books (which I had securely hidden under my bed). I also used this time to begin to learn to channel.

At that point, I didn't have much of an idea who I thought God was. I knew that a god probably existed, but I had NO CLUE what he was, why he was, and how God had anything to do with a BAD person like me. I didn't have enough info to believe blindly in something that I had no proof of. I had spent many years of my life happy in my Christian groups, but that was mostly due to my just being social with positive, happy people that talked about positive, happy stuff all the time. I didn't actually believe that it was because of a MAN named Jesus who said He was God that died for us. That was just too much for me to believe. I would wonder, *How the heck does ONE man dying thousands of years ago wash out all the BAD stuff that people did before and after Him, especially if He never even knew them?*

43

I didn't really think at all about God. The only time that I did, I would cringe because I just knew I was doing the DEVIL'S work by learning to channel. Most of my fascination with channeling at that point was so that I could find and speak with the girl that looked like me and ask WHY she had made me come back after both of those accidents.

That was when I came across an ebook on audio that both my dad and stepdad had suggested I read years earlier, so I downloaded it and listened to the whole thing in one day. The book was called *Conversations with God*, and it absolutely, 100 percent changed my life. The book gave me a belief in God and a new-found understanding of what and who He is. This channeled book told me that even though I had been really, really bad, awful, and horrible to those I loved and horrendously abusive to myself, God still loved me. The book said that there were no such things as good or bad and that it is all relative. It explained that "good" and "bad" are defined by man, for the most part. The book taught that we are all down here to learn lessons from our life circumstances that we planned prior to coming here and to learn from each other. Learning these lessons from each other, the book said, sometimes meant that someone would have to "play the bad guy." To me, that explained so much! (I believe a little differently now, but we can get into that later). After realizing that God was real and that He loved ME, I remember my whole body got covered in goose bumps and I just happy-cried for, like, ten minutes straight! I remember going into the living room where I had the audio playing and turned it to the radio. I still remember the song that was on. It was Madonna's "True Blue" from her *Immaculate Collection* album. When I heard it, I just started jumping up-and-down, spinning, and dancing alone in the living room. I WAS SO HAPPY. For the first time in my life, I knew I was GENUINELY HAPPY!

My passion for channeling continued after this realization, but my focus switched from channeling another being to channeling my soul. This was for the simple reason that I believed in God now, and I believed that I actually had a soul to channel. The books I read about channeling liked to refer to the soul as our higher self. This triggered the memory of the book I'd originally bought when I ordered *Opening to Channel*. This book was called *Becoming Your Higher Self*. I found the book, opened it, and threw myself into it completely. What I mean by that is I REALLY began to practice what they teach in my everyday life. The book teaches that we are SPIRITS living a human experience and the authors explain that by becoming aware of this higher consciousness, which is the true authentic SELF (the REAL us), we are able to clearly see what direction we are to be heading toward. I was quickly learning that by tapping into and becoming our higher self, our lower self (ego, intellect, emotions) just become tools that our higher self is equipped with so we can live a successful human experience while down on this planet.

Finding this out was another turning point in my life. The "Miss Know-It-All" in me was now able to recognize, admit to people, and then apologize when she did lousy things that either hurt them without even realizing it until after the fact. I remember thinking at that time that when I just wasn't being a very nice person, my mind could say, *Oh, it wasn't my fault, it was my lower self's fault!* It sounds REALLY silly now, but that is what I thought then and, surprisingly, for some VERY STRANGE reason it brought a huge amount of humility into my personality. Prior to this, I had NONE, not one sliver! I know now that our lower and higher selves are all one, but the belief that they were separate was what I needed to believe at that time in order to acknowledge the not-so-wonderful qualities within me and begin to change them. Just as I teach all my students now, we can't change until we acknowledge that there is something that needs to be changed.

The biggest surprise to me, my family, my friends, and even my coworkers was that I actually started admitting when I was wrong instead of arguing a point that I knew was wrong. I would do this to win an argument so as to make the other person look stupid so I could look better than them. I began thinking before I spoke and did less of blurting out the first thought that came to my head in any given situation. Knowing about integrating my higher self into my life really slowed me down a great deal. Everyone around me started to notice.

I took this as a sign of encouragement and got up the guts to call my dad and tell him about all the wonderful stuff I had learned about God. Our conversation was short and pretty uncomfortable, but I felt good letting him know that I was aware of what I had done to him and others that I loved and that I was grateful to have God in my life. I heard from him a couple of weeks later via email. He asked me to come over to his house for Father's Day. I was soooooo excited! I couldn't believe it. My dad was actually going to be talking to me again!! My life felt so complete! Little did I know it would become even more complete that night.

Jeff happened to be out of the country the night that I got the email from my dad, so I was unable to call and tell him all about it. I had secluded myself so much in the last two years that I really didn't have anyone to call and tell, so, for some reason, I decided that it was the perfect time to do a meditation and work on my channeling. The session turned into a five-hour meditation in front of the web cam on my Mac laptop. I always recorded the channeling sessions in hopes that I would catch something on tape or hear myself say something that I was not consciously aware of while I was meditating.

About five hours in (which seemed like thirty minutes), I felt the presence of another being. I REALLY, REALLY liked it. I was not scared or creeped out at all, which is strange to me now. You would think that I would have flipped out, but I didn't. Feeling this being that was in the living room with me was such an AMAZING FEELING. I had never felt something quite like it. Every time I would try to explain what it felt like to the video camera, it would go away. I knew that I needed to remember this feeling, so I immediately thought to grab a paper and pen so that I could write it down. From the time I was a little girl, I LOVED writing in my diary and still greatly enjoyed journaling, so that is what I grabbed and began writing in. I didn't want to forget the feeling I was having. I knew, just like a dream, that the things that happen in meditation fade as you come back to reality.

As I described this Being in my journal, I started HEARING thoughts in my head that were not mine! I thought I was going crazy at first, but then laughed and thought: *Well, after five hours of meditation, I am probably going crazy, but this is fun, so I am going to roll with it!* I still have the journal and web cam files from that night when the Being that I was FEELING began to write through me, using my hand and my thought patterns to describe what it had to say to me. This Being said her name was Alana and that she was here to help me raise my vibration so that I could speak with my higher self. She said that my higher self was at such a higher frequency that I would not be able to channel her directly and that she would be helping me get to that point through writing. Alana said she was going to teach me about myself and she would answer any questions I had for her.

With an even more excited outlook on life, I began secretly writing with Alana every night, but I asked the same thing every time we talked. *Who am I? Who are you? Why am I here? What is my reason for life? When will I get to talk to my higher self?*

Alana patiently gave me the same answers every night. What's funny is I never thought to ask anything different. Due to the fact that I now had a relationship with Alana, I got into research mode again. I started learning about automatic writing (which is what I was doing) and read about how Alana could be writing through me. Some websites said that the Beings were angels. Other sites said that she was a fragment of my subconscious mind expressing itself through writing. With my skeptic and logical mind, I was a little more comfortable with the "subconscious" theory and continued studying it from that frame of thinking but it didn't FEEL correct. This felt like so much more than my mind, it felt too beautiful to be so simple.

I had a realization one day that since I believed in God now and believed that I was a Soul/Spirit, why shouldn't I believe in angels now, too? I began some different research this time and through this, I found people familiar with channeling, automatic writing, and communication with Beings from the other side. They didn't call Alana an angel; they called her a spirit guide. I asked Alana if she was the only spirit guide for everyone, and she responded that every person on the planet has several and said she was only one of mine. In fact, she never claimed to be a spirit guide. She always described herself as a Master Teacher. (Later down the road my higher self, guides, and new teachers, some of whom I still work with today, would replace her.)

My life had become so wonderful since I started on my path of self-discovery. Not only was my dad back in my life, but I was back working at the office we had built together. Business was good, Jeff and I were happily living in our house in Carlsbad, and I had my driver's license back. My life was a DREAM come true! I was SO happy and LOVED learning more about this new spiritual passion I had found. The only thing in my life that was not completely perfect was my physical condition. With all the accidents I had been in and my lack of

48

healthy habits through most of my early twenties, my back and neck were in bad shape. I don't think my lungs were very healthy, either, and I just plain didn't have a healthy lifestyle. I didn't eat vegetables, all I ate was fast food, and I didn't drink ANY water, but drank Diet Coke like it was going out of style. Looking back, it is so gross, but the consciousness level I was at back then was cool with it.

One day my back was really killing me. I had four real estate deals going south and I was dealing with multiple homeowners on the phone or via text and email. I decided that I had to get out of the office for at least fifteen minutes. My plan was to go across the street to Moonlight Beach, kick off my three-inch heels, take my suit jacket off, and just relax for fifteen minutes before going back into the war zone that I called my office. But when I pulled out of our parking lot, something (or someone) told me to go right instead of left. Before I knew it, I found myself parked in front of a local yoga studio. I had been there once before and wasn't sure why I was there now. But when I heard Alana's voice in my head (which I was now hearing twenty-four hours a day), she suggested I go in.

I said hi to the girl working there and told her how calming their place was and asked if I could just sit on their couch. She smiled real big and said, *"Of course!"* We started some casual conversation and after telling her that a part of my job was to help people avoid foreclosure she began telling me her situation. She was going through some stressful, scary stuff. She had NO idea how to handle her home and was on the brink of losing it to foreclosure. I helped her with some tips on how to save it as she thanked me over and over and over. Time had come to get back to the office so I got up off the couch. As I got up, I grunted from my back pain and said, "Sheesh, you would never guess that I am only thirty-one with all the pain I deal with." She got a look on her face, grabbed a flyer, and said, "Well, now I get to help YOU!" She invited me to something called Yoga with Reiki that night and didn't charge me for it. I didn't practice yoga back then the way I do now and if I did do it, I preferred the "hot yoga" that was a work out as opposed to a spiritual practice. She saw that I was not excited, but she urged me to come and promised I would love it.

Surprisingly, five hours later, I actually went back! I got there that night all decked out and ready for a workout. I walked into the room and found all these VERY calm people spread out across the studio with blankets and pillows on top of their yoga mats. I was confused, but I went to the back of the room, grabbed some pillows, and marched right up to the front of the class so I could be sure to hear everything the teacher was saying. I set my stuff up.

The yoga class began. My back was killing me but my type A competitive personality kept going. Then, while I was in one of the poses that we were to hold for five minutes, a lady came over and laid her hands on my lower back. She laid them on the EXACT spot that my pain was. She kept her hands there for about two minutes, and when she walked away, THE PAIN WAS GONE! I couldn't believe it! After class, I ran up to the teacher and asked what the heck that lady did to my back to make it better. The yoga teacher explained that the ladies walking around the studio during class were doing Reiki energy healing on all of the students. In my head, I heard Alana say, *Ask her if you can learn to do Reiki on yourself.* I took Alana's suggestion and the very next week, I was in a private training with this yoga teacher and my soon to be Reiki Master learning about the Art of Healing.

Marisa's Story – Part 3
What?! I'm a healer and a medium too?

I had NO idea what Reiki was when I signed up for it, but I showed up to my first day of class SUPER excited. I had my four attunements to the healing energy over the two days that we met. I honestly didn't feel a thing, so I was a little disappointed. But I was feeling good about learning self-healing, more about the ego, tons about the aura, and a bit about divinity. Some of the stuff, I felt I already knew, but it was great to get official training rather than just teaching myself through books and the Internet. My Reiki Master told me that I was to do a twenty-one-day cleanse. What that meant was that I needed to meditate for an hour every day, drink a gallon of water per day, and do the self-healing treatment that I had just learned to do on myself for thirty minutes each day. She also told me to keep a journal about the changes I would be feeling. At the time, I doubted I would feel any changes. I had already changed so much; I couldn't imagine what else could happen to make my life any more complete. I was thrilled with life for the first time EVER.

Over the next twenty-one days, I did everything she told me to do. I really did feel changes. I felt that I had discipline in my life now. I felt a sense of renewal that I had never felt before. I was excited to go back and take Reiki 2 and see what other amazing things I would experience. The second degree of Reiki taught me how to do healings on other people. I learned more about the chakras, the aura, and about how energy effects on us on a daily basis. I was attuned that day to the second level, and then I was done. I had another twenty-one-day cleanse with the same requirements, except this time I was supposed to also practice on others when possible. I already had a few people lined up for the following week. I was excited! I practiced on a few people from work, and they all said that they felt amazing. I was surprised to realize that when I was doing their healing I was also hearing messages, much like the ones I got while I was doing automatic writing, but they were from the other person's guides and angels. The messages were correct every time. I was thrilled! Not only could I write with angels and guides, but now I could talk to other people's guides and help them change their lives the way that my guides helped me to change mine. I felt SO blessed! My life was perfect.

I continued to practice Reiki on people between doing my other work in real estate and mortgage lending, and I also went to every single class I could find on angels, channeling, and healing. I was starting to get a routine down. I practiced on people and even got the confidence to start asking for a donation. People were more than happy to pay. With the first $300 in addition to a $250 dollar "investment in my future" from my mom, I went and bought a Reiki table. I still remember the day. I was so proud!

A few months later, life was still great, but I had no idea my life was about to forever change AGAIN. On Easter Sunday, 2011, I was taking a nice bath with lavender, doing a meditation, and then my self-healing treatment. It felt so good to just relax because I was still working twelve hours a day in real estate doing short sales, dealing with negotiators at banks, and mortgage lending on top of that. But today was Easter, and all the banks were closed and my phone was not ringing. I had nothing to worry about. During my bath, my mind began wandering and I started thinking about Easter and what it was all about. I had come to the belief in the Christ consciousness, in God, and in angels and guides, but I still couldn't get myself to believe that a man who walked this earth was God. I couldn't understand how people could pray to Him if He was just like us. I also couldn't understand how one man dying could wipe away all the sins of every man who lived before and after him. This was too much of a stretch for me.

While I was pondering these things, I heard my higher self's oh-so-familiar voice. Usually, I would only hear her voice while I was doing automatic writing, but this time it came loud and clear without my paper and pen in hand. I was really excited to hear her so clearly. I asked what she had to tell me

You are wondering who Christ is, she said, *so I am here to tell you*. Then she asked me if I truly believed that she was my higher self, that we were one, and that I, Marisa, was simply a human version of her living on the planet to learn lessons and enjoy physicality. "ABSOLUTELY!" I said. She quickly continued with a very simple statement that forever changed me. She said, *you do not have to worship Jesus the man. He is a human spirit just as you are, living in a physical human body, just as you are. Just as I am your higher self, He has a higher self too. His higher self IS Christ. It is His higher self, Christ, that may be worshiped if you would like. It is His actions and teachings as a human that you may learn by*. Basically she said that Jesus was the physical version of Christ (God) and He came to teach us humans how to live lives that we would enjoy and cherish, not only on the earth plane, but also to teach us on the other side that with our free will we can strive to be like Christ and feel the glory and bliss that comes with it.

I was amazed at how simple it was. She had just explained to me who Jesus was, and it touched my heart. Suddenly, so many things made sense, and in an instant, I realized that I finally believed in Jesus! I truly understood who He was and why He was here. It all made sense! I was SO happy; I jumped out of the bath, dried off, and called my dad. I told him all about it and I also told him that I would start coming to church with him because now I understood what the pastors were talking about. I was so happy.

The next day, I was with my boyfriend and told him all about what had happened. As usual, he was very supportive and happy for me. Then I offered to give him a Reiki healing on my new table. My boyfriend (now my fiancé) was the very first healing I ever gave months back and he immediately loved how it made him feel. After that, any chance he had at getting his energy cleared, he jumped at it.

A few days later, Jeff asked for another healing. After I cleared the energy in the room and said my prayer asking the archangels to surround the house and for the Christ Light to shield us from anything that was not for our highest and best good, I felt a little different. But I just figured I was tired and didn't think too much about it. About ten minutes into the healing, the whole room turned into sparkles, and when I looked at Jeff, his physical body looked like a picture on the old TVs when the channel was fuzzy and there were black and white dots everywhere. Amazed at what I was seeing, I asked him if he could see the sparkles and dots, too. He said the room looked normal to him.

Although it seemed crazy that I was seeing this, I was not afraid, so I just went along with it and continued to do the treatment. When I got down to his solar plexus, I heard a train whistle off in the distance and immediately thought it was the train we lived near in Carlsbad. Then, about a minute later and to my utter amazement, I saw WITH MY EYES OPEN a HUGE train pull into our living room, hiss to a stop, and a lady with a briefcase step off. She was wearing a fifties business suit and one of those hats with a veil. She looked very proper and professional, and for some reason I still was not scared. I had been doing automatic writing with angels now for two years and had been hearing them during Reiki healings for over six months. I just assumed that an angel had finally decided to appear, but was showing herself like a regular person to get some point across.

The lady started talking in a foreign language that I didn't understand, so I tried writing down the words she spoke and spelling them phonetically. It looked like German to me, and we later found out that it was. At the time, though, I thought; *I can't understand you*, and she immediately said: *Oh, sorry, I forgot you still only know English*. Then she said: *Let him know that they would have never guessed that I made it here, but let him know I am in Heaven*. She looked at Jeff with a happy tear in her eye, and then she got back on the train as it hissed and then pulled away. This was SO WEIRD. I relayed the message to him, and he said he had no clue what the "angel" was talking about, so we just dropped it.

54

A couple days later, his parents happened to come into town to spend a late Easter with us. We had a fabulous day together with yummy food, and somehow Jeff's grandmother came up in conversation while talking to his mom. I think she had made a dish with a recipe that was given to her by Jeff's grandmother. We were told that grandma was German and a pretty strict mother. She was an atheist and would sometimes cause issues when Jeff's dad was growing up because her husband would want to take the kids to church and she wouldn't allow it. We were also told she was a successful career woman that worked for the railroad company.

When I heard that, it felt like all the blood rushed out of my body. I got totally weak and almost passed out. The image of a German woman, in a business suit, stepping off a train and telling me they never would have thought I made it here flashed through my head. For the first time in two years of automatic writing with angels and guides, I realized that I had accidentally communicated with a DEAD PERSON. I didn't know what to think. I was nervous; the first thing that came to my mind was that SATAN was after me now because I understood who Jesus was. The only thing I could think to do was to call my dad and tell him what was happening. On Sunday, I found myself at the church that we would later get kicked out of.

Marisa (A Father's Take)

Marisa was the perfect child. The center of attention everywhere we went, she was beautiful and very smart and showed leadership qualities. At her pre-school daycare center, she always had to sit at the head of the table at mealtime. It was as if she was in charge. She also did extremely well in school and brought home excellent grades and scholastic honors. In addition, she was a gifted athlete, playing soccer and lettering in softball in high school. She was accepted at my alma mater, the University of California at Santa Barbara, but she had a desire to take a break from school and take a year off and learn how to ski and work to pay her own way. I thought that was a good idea. I thought there would be a good life lesson in there somewhere as long as she came back after a year and pursued her academic studies.

But as we learn in life, nothing is static. Life is dynamic and ever changing. Circumstances put Marisa in the wrong place at the wrong time. Her move away from home took her up to Mammoth Mountain in central California. She ended up residing with about ten other people in a big house that turned out to be more like the movie *Animal House*. Someone led her to smoke a heroin-laced cigarette, and that was all it took to commence a twelve-year nightmare for her mother and me. Here this perfect child was and due to circumstances we wish hadn't occurred, she turned into another person entirely. Eventually, the highs and lows of drug-dependency sent her in and out of the legal system and care homes for drug dependent persons. To look at Marisa today, you would never believe she had become that kind of a person, but even that part of her life (according to "them" up there) fell into the plans Marisa the Spirit had before becoming Marisa the human.

After Marisa completed several tough anti-dependency programs that included probation, her AA sponsor, who owned a mortgage company, suggested that she come to work there. Marisa dove into the mortgage business and became very skilled at being a loan officer. But, soon after becoming successful and dealing with the stress involved in success, my daughter contracted a seizure disorder. It wasn't a simple case of being an epileptic with some straightforward medicine to take care of it. Her disorder was tied to her previous drug addiction. Her brain wasn't functioning the way it should. The frequency of her seizures was getting faster, with seizures happening as close as one a week but no more than twenty-eight days apart. She had met Jeff (her boyfriend) by this time, and now he and I were in constant need of knowing where she was at all times. She eventually totaled five or six cars (I've lost track), and she hurt herself with abrasions and cuts and concussions from air-bag deployments, though she never hurt anyone else. Her seizures had her doctors basically stumped. They put her on a variety of medications that soon became powerful drug cocktails. Just because the medications were legal didn't make things better. Marisa became a prescription drug addict.

By this time, Marisa and I had opened our own real estate and Mortgage Company. This was in late 2005, just when the economy plateaued then took a huge nose dive. That caused a great deal of stress in our lives, as every transaction over the next few years was a critical one. Our emotions were high. I prayed. I prayed a lot. I did a lot of reading, too. I read just about every spiritually uplifting book I could find and discussed them in Bible study classes with my pastor and with other male Christian friends. The Bible study classes were a great help, as there is often comfort in group misery.

Due to her concussions and the danger of being alone with her seizure disorders, Marisa moved out of her condo and into my home with me. This brought added stress into my life. I had become a grown-up baby sitter trying to survive an economy that eventually not only wiped out a life's work of properly investing for retirement, but also had me over $100,000 in credit card debt with 29 percent interest rates. It was a very scary time for me, and watching my grown daughter become more like a child was harder still. I ended up having a stroke. It was only a

TIA (a trans-ischemic attack), which is a mini stroke. As Johnny Bench, the Hall of Fame catcher once said (paraphrasing and replacing the word injury with stroke) *a mini-stroke is what happens to other people, but when it happens to you, it's a major stroke.* It could have indeed become a full blown stroke with permanent after-effects including slurred speech and paralysis, had Marisa not gotten me to the hospital within three hours. I was physically and mentally a total mess by then. It just didn't seem like God was listening to me at all. If He was listening, I kept asking Him to take me home to Heaven.

Marisa and I had reached a point of no return. After she totaled my car again (which had no insurance if she was driving), my emotions shot up high enough for me to tell her that she didn't have a father on earth and if she wanted to have a father, then she should look to her father in Heaven. We shut it down cold turkey. We became estranged. For a year, there was no communication in any form or fashion between us.

I remember the day one year later, on Father's Day, when I welcomed her back into my life as the father seeing his prodigal daughter return. I had received my baby girl back. Her transformation was a gift from God. Marisa had measured my words and had begun the long journey of seeking truth.

She found studying the art of Reiki interesting. It was something that would wake her mind up to another dimension or level of understanding. She became quite good at it and became a certified Reiki healer. She also read about channelers like Edgar Cayce and others who had been able to communicate with the other side. These changes in her life led us to the kind of life that we lead now.

Prior to our reunion, Marisa had experienced a near death experience in one of her car crashes. She had an expensive brand new Mercedes C350 coupe and was coming home from a photo shoot of some kind with cosmetics. She had just exited the freeway. After passing through a light, she went into a seizure and crossed three lanes of traffic after clearing a grassy median. Fortunately, she didn't hit any oncoming traffic, which is usually very heavy at that intersection with the freeway. What she hit was a fire hydrant. One of the paramedics told me she nearly drowned. What Marisa remembers is drowning and seeing the light. She said she'd never felt so much peace in her life. She saw people, but didn't know who they were. It wasn't a long experience, and she didn't go through the light. She remembered very little, which is typical, because it usually took up to one hour after the onset of a seizure for her to come back to the world and know who she is and where she is. While everyone around her was freaked out and stressed out, she always came back in peace. There was peace on the other side, and that's where she felt she was when she had a seizure. As time went on, in fact, it almost seemed like she welcomed the seizures.

About a year after Marisa and I accepted each other as father/daughter again, life began to get better. It had already started to get better for me in 2009 in my work. I was able to eliminate my credit card debt. The two things I had sincerely prayed to God for were peace within and to be debt free. Those two things became my goals. I wanted to live simply and succeeded in doing just that. I live what would be considered by many people to be a great life on a pauper's income and budget. I've figured it out. At least, so far.

By this time, Marisa was reading everything she could find about communicating with angels. She had not been able to consciously cross over after her near death experience. She also discovered automatic writing. She was not into self-hypnosis, and discounting online psychics, most previously documented conversations with the other side were done through hypnotic states.

In April, 2011, Marisa was putting a whole lot of dots together. She was about to understand who Christ was. On Easter morning, she finally figured out that Christ was God. She knew other religions called Christ by other names, but she came to understand that Christ is the perfect *personification* of the Creator of All that we call God. His personification is a part of God in which He gives Himself personality and the ability to procreate Himself. She also understood that He also gave of Himself the knowledge of His existence; this is called the mother, or female, aspect of Him, which is the Holy Spirit. *The Urantia Book* says it is the Holy Spirit that creates the angels. His personification as Christ coupled with the Holy Spirit created souls, billions of souls, which I will touch on shortly.

In her bathtub on that Easter morning in 2011, Marisa realized that Jesus was the direct human personification of Christ. Jesus was the direct spirit from the soul of Christ and in some unknown way to us was put into man on earth. He was God as man and man as God. Marisa had figured it out! She cried uncontrollably and gave her spirit to Christ. She was truly baptized in the spirit. Her honest gift was her giving her free will to Christ the Father. Her life was now new. She had shed her old life. She felt what I felt when she and I had been baptized thirteen years earlier. There was an awakened spirit within her, and things were about to start happening because of it.

Marisa didn't go to church very often. When she did, it was because I asked her to. Organized religion seemed more like a business to her, so it was now early autumn, 2011, when I asked her to accompany me one Sunday morning. The service was a fellowship held in the back yard of the house in which the pastor and his wife lived. They shared the gospel during the sermon. As they spoke, I sat under a tree a little away from the others. I unexpectedly felt someone stroking my head from front to back. I was dumbfounded. The pastor's wife soon noticed my distraction. I was turning my head, looking for whoever was stroking my head, looking up as if something had hit me. Without breaking stride, she continued the sermon.

After I realized that there was no one close enough to touch my head, I whispered what happened into Marisa's ear. She said it was my angel guide. Then she asked me who a particular lady was. She was sitting among many other ladies who were apparently there to console her. I told Marisa I would tell her later who the lady was. But later never came. We were distracted and left separately in our cars shortly after the sermon and brief chats with others.

About two weeks passed. I received a call from Marisa. She said she had been doing a Reiki healing when a young man had appeared in the corner of her studio with one hand on his hip and the other in his pocket. He was leaning against the wall. He was an apparition. Marisa said it wasn't scary, and she didn't even flinch. I would have fainted or had a heart attack, but she had studied enough to know that spirits can be seen by people who have been blessed with a higher energy level than the rest of us. God had given Marisa a new ability after her baptism, a higher energy level.

The young man in the corner had telepathically introduced himself to Marisa as Bill. He asked her to have me tell his wife of nearly fifty years that he couldn't adequately describe the grandness of Heaven, but that he loves her eternally and will be there when she crosses over. Marisa didn't understand all of this, but we figured out that the lady at the church was Bill's wife, the lady that Marisa had asked me about. Marisa had seen sparkles all around her and thought something was wrong with her eyes. Bill next informed Marisa that he saw that she saw him. Marisa hadn't seen him that day at church, only the sparkles around a lady she didn't know was his wife. In fact, Marisa didn't know either one of these people before these events. She had never even seen them or known of their existence. After the Reiki session concluded, she called me and told me what had happened. Then I told her who Bill's wife was, and she relayed the message from Bill that I needed to tell his wife.

I had been going to this church from the time it had been a mega church. Because of the politics of religion, it had shrunk to a small fellowship in their backyard. After twenty-five years of on-and-off attendance however, I had never become a member, even though I had attended several different Bible classes. Now I needed to go to the pastor with this situation. Bill had regularly attended many of the Bible classes I attended and died suddenly at age eight-six of a heart attack. Marisa had now given me a message from a dapper young man by the name of Bill that I needed to relay to his widow. I wanted my pastor's approval, or at least his passive consent.

What I got from him were passages from the Old and New Testaments about the dangers of seeking out mediums and spirits and dealing with the dark side. My pastor was worried about Marisa's and my souls. Marisa was not a medium yet, but she was becoming a spiritual intuitive. She was now living a life bathed in the light of Christ, and yet something very strange had happened to her. I was told—no I was *forbidden* by my pastor to relay the message from Bill. That was unsettling to me, so I asked if he and his wife would meet with Marisa and me to discuss this strange situation over lunch. I was shocked when he said they would not meet with us over the matter. The whole thing was scaring the living daylights out of them. They surely thought Marisa and I had finally gone over the edge. They knew me well and had been there for me when I was going through hell dealing with Marisa's addiction problems, coupled with the eventual end of my marriage. For twelve years, they had witnessed the total disruption of my life.

Although I had been baptized on Marisa's twenty-first birthday in 1998, I had never become a member, though I was a devoted attendee of their congregation. Over the years, and for various reasons, I also attended two more churches. I couldn't get enough learning. I loved all the different sermons I was hearing. I even watched the television evangelists and my car radio was set to the Christian station.

I finally made a decision. When you get physically sick, you go to your medical doctor. When you get spiritually sick you go to your pastor. Marisa had read up on channeling and had met a few people who had succeeded in getting through to the other side. Some are born with this ability, and others, like Marisa, gain it without asking and without warning.

To my ego-based disappointment, my pastor now shunned us. We were basically asked to leave the church and not let the door hit us in the backside on the way out. I decided to go to one more service, but Marisa refused to come. I thought that if Bill's wife were there, I would go ahead and give her Bill's message and let the chips fall where they may. If she wasn't going to be there that Sunday, then the whole matter would be over.

God put her at the service that day. Afterward, she was surrounded by people consoling her. It had been almost six weeks since Bill had passed, and the reality of his passing had truly settled in. She was depressed. She knew he was in Heaven because he was a good man, despite killing many men in three different wars as a Marine. But she was very lonely.

I looked up to the sky and said, "Okay, God, this whole thing is your ballgame. If you want me to talk to her, fine. But if not, then get me out of here for the last time." When I looked at Bill's widow again, she was standing alone, surrounded by rose bushes as though she was one of them. There was no one else there. I couldn't believe it. Where had all her friends gone? The next thing I knew, I was standing in front of her. I said something to the effect that I was so sorry for her loss. She was as limp as a child who's just seen her cat run over by a car. Then I told her that something really crazy happened and that I had a message for her. I told her that the pastor and his wife did not want me to repeat what Marisa had heard and experienced and passed to me, but I felt that I must tell her. So I told her that Marisa had seen Bill. Then I told her what Bill had said.

It was like someone had flipped a switch. At that moment her eyes lit up, her shoulders shot up, and she started crying and laughing at the same time. I thought I was going to have a heart attack. I was looking around, hoping the pastor was nowhere near us. I didn't know what to do. Finally, she stopped crying, and with a huge smile, she kept saying thank you and hugging me. Bill's widow is Korean. She converted to Christianity through Bill when they were married following the Korean War. When she stopped thanking me, she said that Bill had had twenty-four heart stints. (I already knew that from my Bible classes with him.) She said that every time he was on the gurney before surgery, he squeezed her hand and told her that if he went home to Christ, then he would find some way to let her know he was okay and that he would continue to love her eternally. Bill had kept his promise and Marisa was the go between.

I saw her again a few months later as she was headed to a yoga class. She looked happy and gave me a hug. She said she was late and needed to run, but she had a peace about Bill now. I wished her well and Godspeed.

With that experience, a whole new chapter opened up in my life and Marisa's.

Conversations with Angels

Over the next months, and following a sympathetic meeting with a pastor from another church in Solana Beach, California, Marisa's abilities increased exponentially. She was seeing angels who had names and didn't want to be called angels. They said they were messengers and friends from previous lives on earth, former human beings who had died and gone to Heaven. To me, that was getting scary. I was really worried that Marisa was traveling down a slippery slope into the depths of Hell. I was worried that this was Satan's way of trying to win my daughter's soul again. Surely Marisa had lived in Hell during her addictions, and Satan wasn't about to lose her so easily just because she had been baptized in the Light of Christ. But Marisa assured me that she always said the Lord's Prayer and asked that Christ's Light and His shield protect her from the dark side and for His will to be done in her life. I was deeply involved because I wanted to trust my daughter and believe in her, so I encouraged her, and they, our angel guides (Alana, Eden, and Jeremy) encouraged us. They told me about my passion for knowledge and understanding and my ("minimalist", my self- description) ability to write. I was already a writer of a bi-monthly lifestyles column called *Baby Boomer Peace* for *The Coast News* and *The Rancho Santa Fe News* in coastal north San Diego County. But Alana, Eden, and Jeremy, and others were insistent about exposing the Truth, about exposing God to others just like we did with Bill's wife.

When an Angel Tells You to Write a Book, You Write a Book

That book is what Marisa and I decided we'd better write. They told us that the earth and mankind were going through a new dimensional shift that started in November 2011. They said that we humans are creations of our own making from spirit. They said that after November 2011, the earth was being uplifted and beginning to move toward a new dimension. They said that with the energy level of the earth being uplifted, there were going to be many, many people like Marisa whose abilities to sense, feel, or see the other side was going to spike exponentially. They said that in many of these cases, the people being affected would not understand what was happening. They would think they were going crazy and would be prone to suicidal thoughts. One of the testimonials later in this book is about a session with Marisa that revealed just that.

Our guides said that we humans now residing on earth need to understand who God is and why He is who He is and why we are what we are. They said that if Marisa and I wrote this book and were able to save even one soul, then our effort would be a success.[1] They didn't want us to write this book for fame or fortune; however, they said that many people will say things like, "Oh, that's just another Christian book," and skeptics will say, "Marisa is having hallucinations arising from her past substance abuse." They said there will be many skeptics. But they also said that this book will come into the hands of those who are lost and weary. For them, *"Answers"* will like a cool breeze on a hot summer day. Marisa and I are attempting to turn what they call *"teaching quantum physics to kindergarteners"* into understandable language. We already knew through our experience with our pastor that this work would be tough to do, especially when dealing with the dogmas of religion.

On a side note, I initially had this as a footnote:

Alana, Eden, and others give support to what is called by most New Age and Spiritualists, the Higher Self. They say that

---

[1] Since the commencement of this book, Marisa has healed many wounded Souls.

my Higher Self in reality is me. But that's really hard to understand because when I pray, I just pray to the "Lord". To me "lord" means God and anyone else up there that can hear me and guide me and be for my highest and best here on earth in this lifetime. It's all those "guys" up there who help me connect with God so that my petitions really will be heard.

Hopefully, I'll be able to explain the "guys up there" a little better as I go along. But in the meantime, I'm going to bug my daughter and use the word, Lord. Please don't be offended when I conflate the terms. As they said, this is like quantum physics boiled down to its lowest common denominator: me...you...why?

Marisa cringes when I say "lord" in reference to our Higher Self. But I explained to her that whenever things happened in the Bible, it was the Lord (this is the term the translator of the Authorized Version used) that came through. It got to the point that anyone of authority in those days could be called lord. Lord referred to something or someone of a higher authority. When the prophets came in contact with angels that took on human form, the prophets called them Lord. This was true even in the time of Sodom and Gomorrah, when the "lords," or "angels," appeared to Lot to tell him to gather up his family and leave before the destruction of those two cities (and maybe Atlantis?). Even the Jews in the time of the Exodus were protected in their homes by lords and angels from the death of the first-born children when they were told to paint their door jambs red with blood. Angels of the Lord helped the apostles walk apparently between time and freed them from prison when they were chained behind well secured bars and guards. They just vanished and reappeared in the town square somehow. Isaiah spent the entirety of his book in the Old Testament seeing and speaking to the "Lord" who was giving him prophesies.

So please excuse me ahead of time if, like Marisa, you prefer me not to include "myself" or my "higher self" as Lord because that would be like praying to myself. But when you do pray, when you ask that His will be done, which is like turning on your computer in the morning, your higher self goes about with absolute authority, respecting your free will, and does all things possible to steer you on your predetermined path. Throughout the book, just note that "higher self" and "lord" are interchangeable to me. Since I am a piece of God, I am the spirit of the Soul of myself, the higher self, living in this earthly animal (we're just civilized animals now), and my "Higher Self" is a piece of Himself (Spirit). When in Spirit I set this life up, but now as human with amnesia I don't remember setting my life up by design in advance with the approval of my Soul and Christ: "God's Plan." The overriding goal, I've learned, is to find God in this life. That's pretty much it. Not just in blind faith, but to really know God and just how big He is and yet how small He is too. He built the Universes but lives in me, too. How crazy is that?

Eventually, in future books, we will be able to present answers to mysteries of the earth that our angel guides are willing to reveal to us, despite their both saying they are not that good at earth history. They said they would bring us other experts in that area to help us.

In the past, whenever anyone tried to explain the hereafter to me or if I picked up a New Age book on the subject, my eyes glazed over and I quickly lost interest. It just seemed "out there". Generally the people who are really into this subject seem to be writing in a foreign language. When the guides and angels began communicating with us, they sometimes got very technical. "But I don't understand," I told them. Then I told them about the American essayist and satirist H.L. Mencken (1880–1956), who coined the term "boobus americanus." What I believe "boobus americanus" means is, in essence, the same as KISS—"keep it simple stupid." I wasn't calling them stupid, but I asked them to give this tough subject to me in "boobus americanus" terms so that I would be able to understand and keep it simple in this book for people like me to understand.

Furthermore, I said I could not write this book unless I knew that there were consequences for evil behavior, so we will touch on the yang of God's creation, which is Hell and where it is and how we in this very day are experiencing a tumultuous battle between good and evil. On February 12 and 26, of 2012, Marisa and I turned on the cassette tape machine and started taping our sessions together.

We learned a great deal. We learned many of the answers that I had been eager to hear. As our angel guides said, this is quantum physics being taught to a kindergartner, but they were still able to convey the basic structure of God, who is absolutely everything including the paper this book is printed on. The word "complex" is too simple a word to describe God, but what we are most concerned with is dealing with the personality side of God, call that whatever you like but "they" call Him the Christ and more appropriately, the Light. Christ filters down through the cosmos, all the way down to me, as a spirit and then as human with Him inside me.

Some Answers: Part 2

What is *Some Answers*?

We are all spirit, and Heaven is home and where we started from.[2] We have all lived before and we will live forever. Our eternal lives are a series of growths, a series of experiences we must live through until we can sit at the right hand of Christ. While in Heaven, we choose to come to earth again. You and I design a life that will have us live a human existence and allow us to experience predetermined life lessons. We choose who and what we want to be when entering the human vessel and its earthly mind and ego (brain) and, for better or worse, our human free will.

Each of us as spirit sat down in Heaven with our guides to plan a life that will give us the ability to learn the lessons we need to learn in order for our Soul to grow. After a plan has been designed with our guides, it is taken to and approved by our Soul and Christ. We also confer with members of our Soul Group and Soul Family because they are almost always a continuing part of our life plans. In a future book, we will be writing about the approval process in more depth, including how body, human family, location, etc., are all predetermined.

My life was designed for me to pursue my highest and best good on earth. It's a life designed in a way that I can learn lessons that allow my Soul to grow. For example, in addition to trying to "find God," I might assign myself another lesson, to truly love myself. Another assignment might be to learn to set

---

[2] Jeremy: Earth, too, is Heaven. Many who are attuned to the right energy can experience Heaven right here on earth, whereas others whose energies are misdirected will experience hell on earth. We want to stress that Jesus was home to and came from the soul known as Christ, the second soul following the Holy Spirit, which makes up the Trinity. As humans, we are all our soul and the soul has the "spirit," which is the Holy Spirit living within it.

(A long teaching session followed this with teachings regarding the structure of the universes and the dimensions which we can cover in future book(s).)

boundaries. Another might be to be rich and philanthropic, or poor and humble. All our experiences are designed to glorify God with the ultimate goal of discovering the Light of God within us and learning to live a life of peace and love without being a detriment to someone else. It's a great plan. But because of our free will, we do a great job of trying to muck up a plan we don't remember making. It is our lineage above us and our other heavenly friends that we've asked along for help who have the tough job of trying to keep us on our plan…on *"God's Plan"*.

God is everything. Christ is the created personality of God. The Holy Spirit creates the angels and is also a permeating spirit within the soul of every human, which gives us the ability to understand and have knowledge of God. When speaking of Christ or the Holy Spirit, we are talking about the human aspect of God; the personality, the knowledge of Him and the likeness. There is one little caveat when deciding to become human again, though. We come as *amnesiacs*. We do not remember that we are spirit or much more. We don't remember God's plan for us. Even worse, we are born amnesiacs in a world that is deeply influenced by evil forces. There is a spiritual war going on.

Stick with me here. As they said, we are kindergarteners. We think linearly, so, dimensionally, earth is "roughly" at the same level as the top of or the first of seven layers of Hell. Hell just happens to have seven levels, just as God's Heaven has seven levels. Level One of Hell means you've almost escaped but Level Seven of Heaven is the top. Unfortunately for us, hell and earth are in the domain of the warlike Soul of Lucifer, who also created his own form of the Holy Spirit, and that is Satanism. I will expound on Lucifer and Satan later in this book. Dimensionally, earth and the highest level of Hell are only separated by that first layer of what we experience as Heaven that we all pass through on the way to eternity after we die or cross over. They call this layer of existence the Etheric Realm. The Etheric Realm is where we all go first after dying. It is the first step toward reaching what we call heaven. Lots of stuff goes on in that Realm.

71

This was told to Marisa and me in a Reiki session followed by two ensuing taped conversations. During my first Reiki session, my dad appeared in the room with us. That was our first recording. I didn't have a clue that he was there, but Marisa said he looked like he was about twenty-one and was playing catch with a baseball with someone she couldn't see. All she could hear was the pop of the glove. My dad was wearing the Dodger jacket that my brothers wanted him buried in, since he was such a lover of the Los Angeles Dodgers. He was happy and smiling.

My mom came in, too. She had their favorite dog, Buttons, from their elder years in her arms. My mom looked about thirty, with flowing blonde hair. Her first words in twelve years were to tell me to stop smoking. Since I smoke cigars, I guess I should give them up, but I always think of George Burns. His doctors kept telling him to quit, and he went to all of their funerals and lived to be 100. I said, "Geez, Mom, I don't see you for twelve years and the first thing you do is scold me?" She said she couldn't help it. A mother is always a mother. Isn't that so true? I guess we just never stop being parents even after going home to heaven.

My dad was surprised that I had inquired about him. He thought I had enough anger toward him that I wouldn't care if he was safe and having a good time in Heaven or not. I wasn't sure why he felt that way, except that we just weren't very close because of his schedule, my having three brothers, and my leaving home at the age of seventeen. I had to carry a burdensome secret about him because my name is the same as his, but I learned to do it. It was something my mom told me before I boarded a plane to San Diego from Taiwan, where we lived at the time. I was still a kid and heading out to live on my own, and she said I had to know that my father had had an affair that created, of all things, exactly what my mom wanted and never got, a little girl. I had a half-sister. But I couldn't tell my brothers or confront my dad about it. My dad certainly learned that I knew of this when he returned to Heaven. I suppose he wrongly assumed I had no interest in knowing anything more about his welfare after he died.

I was nervous that Satan was just being sly in relaying these messages that we were now taping. During my time as a devoted Christian, it has been preached to me over and over again that Satan is the great deceiver. But both Marisa and I know that Jesus said, "Seek and you will find, ask and you shall receive." Before starting any session, Marisa always says the Lord's Prayer and then goes into a simple conversation with Christ, asking Him to protect us from evil with His Light, His Love, and His Shield. Marisa and I both believe that there is no way God will turn His back on us when we're asking for that kind of protection from evil.

My mother died in 2001, just before 9/11, which would have either killed her or revitalized her. She hated anyone who hated our country. Eleven years ago, when my three brothers and I were going through our parents' personal possessions after Mom passed away, we discovered a Bronze Star given to my father during World War II. Our father had never told us that he'd received such a distinguished honor. It had bothered us ever since we'd found it. I thought if this was really my dad who popped in, then he would know why he'd received the medal and why he hadn't told any of us about it. If I didn't know, Marisa wouldn't have had a clue.

The first thing he said was that he loved us all greatly. He also said that being a parent was tough for him because he always thought he was never going to live past the age of twenty-six. He definitely didn't think he was going to go to Heaven. He said that he did things in his life that he wasn't proud of and therefore didn't want to think of God until he was closing in on his death. Then he said that God is a loving and forgiving God. He said that Heaven is beyond description, but that he was improving himself by being "in college" up there. He didn't tell us, nor did I ask, what kind of classes he was taking, but he said he likes playing on the school's baseball team and that he plays third base and sometimes pitches. He confused me when he said

Heaven can be whatever we want it to be. I responded with this question: If Heaven is whatever you want it to be, then does he always pitch no-hitters and hit grand slam home runs every time he's up? What would be so much fun in that? He said that if that was the desire, then that would be the outcome, but all his buddies in Heaven that he chooses to play with play by the competitive spirit just as they did when they were human. He said he had a good batting average—close to .400—but his pitching earned run average wasn't too good.

During World War II, my father was in the Army Air Force and was hunkered down with his unit. He became a commissioned officer after going to OCS school (with Clark Gable, of all people) in Florida immediately following the attack on Pearl Harbor. He had entered the Army Air Corps after high school and had already served five years and become a staff sergeant before being commissioned. He was not a pilot, but part of his job was being a nose or tail gunner in the B-15s. My dad said that within the first year of the war, three quarters of his buddies from school and from his former stateside company were already dead. He said that within three months of serving in England after his commission that ninety percent of his buddies had been shot down by Nazi planes. He said he hated the war, but he did his job to the best of his ability because he believed in the greatness of our country. He believed that our country was fighting evil that needed conquering. He eventually learned that evil is seen in the eye of the beholder. The angels and my dad both said that for evil to be evil there has to be the intent to be evil, to actually be evil in the eyes of God. My dad didn't kill for the sake of killing. He killed America's enemies because he felt he and so many other Americans were fighting for something much greater than themselves.

When a Nazi sniper was taking out my dad's friends and fellow soldiers, my dad found a way to get close enough to get the sniper in his sights. Just as he was going to pull the trigger and blow the enemy's head off, the sniper and my dad locked eyes. My dad said that he saw those eyes every day for the rest of his life. He was living a nightmare. He had done the right thing, but in his heart, he was responsible for taking another person's son, brother, uncle, or father. My dad was like almost every soldier who came back from that war. They didn't talk about it. They were all living in their own Hells. My dad said that dropping bombs from 20,000 feet was so much different than holding a rifle and seeing someone's eyes. From the air, it was just annihilation of everyone and everything in the bomb's path, and he just didn't give it much thought. Seeing another man's eyes was something different.

Even though my three brothers and I served our country in different branches of the military, we never had to encounter what our dad did. While raising us, he didn't want to talk about killing and putting ourselves in harm's way. I guess he was trying to protect us from a similar fate. He won the Bronze Star, but it wasn't something he was proud of, despite saving the lives of many of his fellow soldiers.

He said he is not regretful of how he treated us as a father. He apologized for being the way he was, which was a physical disciplinarian, but that there are no regrets in Heaven. Emotions are for the most part limited to human feelings. Humans are earthly vessels that are filled with our own spirit. Not even our guides know fully how God pulls that off, but we live a life of fight or flight as earthly humans. (I'll discuss this later.) Humans contain a mind, a body, a spirit, and an ego. Part of the mind is our true eternal personality, but it's only a part of it because we are mostly chemicals and earthly products and, as they said, sometimes the chemicals in us go haywire when coupled with our free will.

Because we have designed and mandated amnesia, we don't know we're spirit (that small piece of our much larger Soul living inside of us trying to speak to us), so we rely upon our mind and our ego to make decisions. Without including God in the equation by sharing our free will, we make all kinds of mistakes. We make these mistakes when we are aging, when we are getting married, when we are raising a family and children.

75

We designed a plan to be the families we are, but by design we don't remember the plan, so we stumble our way through life. But if we turn our will over to God's huge administration looking after us, then it is possible to find the ultimate peace and happiness we are looking for. There are lessons to be learned, too. Earth is a great place for our souls to learn lessons and grow by allowing a small piece of His self to become our spirit.

My mom liked to play bridge. That is the card game she and my dad loved to play when they were alive on earth. Her best friend in Heaven is my Aunt Claire. I thought that was odd because my mom was Christian Science, and my dad's sister, Aunt Claire, was a fire-breathing Baptist. Short of eating, breathing, and constant prayer, my aunt saw just about everything else as a sin. My mom had such disdain for her while they were both on earth, so their being best friends in Heaven was certainly a good sign in my mind.

My mom grew up in a family that didn't have to struggle in the Great Depression because my grandfather worked for a book company that provided books to schools. My dad's past is very murky, however, and he never spoke of it. My mom was primarily English, my dad, Italian. In those days, the English hated the Italians and (typically) vice versa. Nonetheless, they met just four months before the war broke out and then hurried to get married three weeks later as my dad left for the war. My mother and father didn't even see each other for four years. Can you imagine that? And then they stayed married for nearly fifty years. That is amazing, considering everything they went through in the ensuing years. Apparently that was their life plan.

My mom and my dad are from the same Soul Family and, more specifically, from the same Soul Group which is a subgroup of the Family. According to Eden, from our super-huge Soul that (believe it or not) is really you (you'll see some day) there are seven to fifteen members of a Soul Group and around 150 in a Soul Family and about 1,500 in a soul Pod. They likened a Pod to a university, where the Soul Pod learns its lessons together through time. Those numbers can move around, depending upon our Soul's free will and whether our individual Soul is ambitious or lazy. Yes, laziness even exists in Heaven. Nevertheless, my parents have apparently lived together three times as husband and wife and at times as brother and sister.

Because my parents loved traveling here on earth, they do it extensively in Heaven too. My parents like to go see what's going on. They can't adequately describe what they do when they get to wherever they are going, but in a future book I will find out as much as I can about the various places we can live after we've moved on from this life. It will be a lot of fun to learn more about the structure and features of the heavenly universes, but they said a foundation had to be poured first in this book.

After hearing all of this, Alana (who was really channeling Jeremy) and Eden asked if I had any questions. This was taking place when the U.S. presidential campaign was starting up in early 2012, and I was very unhappy about the direction our country was going in. I mentioned to the angels that I was sure the Founding Fathers were rolling over in their graves if they could only see how the Constitution was being dismissed as a dusty old piece of fabric. I was reminded that no one is in their graves, however to my utter astonishment my daughter said that Benjamin Franklin had come in. She said my mom was poking my dad in the ribs and pointing. Apparently there are celebrities in Heaven. I wasn't skeptical at all though. I was thrilled! But, typical of me, I immediately went brain dead and didn't have a single question I could formulate.

Benjamin Franklin proceeded to let me know that everything that happens is God's plan. He said that even the earth has a soul and that our country, the United States, has a soul. He said that the United States was founded on the respect and honor of God and that they intended to keep it that way. He said that mankind's free will causes leaders to forget God and make human decisions that are not always best for the people, but that God continues to try to clean up the mess left behind. He also said that there is no time in Heaven. He said that 1776 was occurring simultaneously with my conversation with him in 2011. I didn't understand that at all. That's when I told Marisa that we'd better tape these sessions so that we could listen to them again in order to better understand what they were trying to teach us and why.

"Why us?" was my constant refrain. As we ended the session, I couldn't help blurting out that I couldn't wait to write in my newspaper column that I had spoken to Benjamin Franklin. Mr. Franklin calmly said that if I did, then everyone would think I was a "crackpot". My daughter looked at me with a raised eyebrow, so I decided that wasn't such a good idea. I asked if I could spend future sessions interviewing the Founding Fathers. Mr. Franklin said yes, but that it was his understanding that it was necessary for Marisa and me to first prove their existence and their ability to communicate with us. Eden said I should only write what is true and explain it in as elemental a fashion as humanly possible. Paraphrasing Jesus, "A house built on sand will not stand." It is necessary to explain the foundation of the lineage of God to man before we try to explain everything else. Otherwise, everything else just wouldn't make sense.

I love the mysteries of our earth. Our angel guides have already said that I can ask whatever questions I want and they will give us the answers. I wish I could reveal one mystery right now, but these sessions will be in future books. I think our second book will be on the structure of the universe, and then the third book will delve into earth's mysteries, such as the Pyramids and other mind-boggling structures. In a fourth book, I'm determined to interview the souls of Benjamin Franklin and George Washington. I'm really looking forward to that!

This book is our attempt to try to explain who we are and why we are here in the simplest way possible. Marisa and I pulled out the old cassette tape recorder and the more up-to-date electronic recording devices when we began taping. As of this writing, we now have upwards of 100 hours of conversational recordings and they're growing every week. It's a lot of fun now that I trust that it is Christ-inspired and not the work of Lucifer. I'm convinced of that.

Our First Two Tapings
Summarized in My Own Words
February 12 and 26, 2012

Marisa saged the room and then said the Lord's Prayer. She then asked Christ to surround us in His Light and His Shield. Then we turned on the cassette recorder and started talking.

Marisa has a gift that most clear channelers don't have. She does not have to be put in a trance or be in a hypnotic state to communicate with the other side. She sees angels and dead people when they want to be seen. Although she can never guarantee that passed loved ones or angels will make their presence available to her, they always seem to. When they appear, most of the time they don't immediately nor telepathically communicate. There is a reason for that, but we aren't sure what it is. We think it has something to do with people's energy levels. Nonetheless, some people come through and just start jabbering, whereas others have to use pantomime and body language to communicate with and through Marisa.

One day in 1974, my wife and I were sitting on a beach reading an old *Reader's Digest* when we came to an article on Chinese astrology that explained that the word "astrology" is a misnomer because Chinese astrology had nothing to do with the stars other than using them to determine the time of year. Six thousand years ago, the Chinese decided to start keeping track of people's personality traits based on their birthdates. They also found that there are both differences and similarities in cycles and in personalities in the days of the year. There are five cycles of twelve years in a complete cycle of sixty years. Then it starts over again. The Chinese determined that if a baby is born in the sixtieth year of a senior family member's lifetime, the elder will be the child's mentor because they have so much in common. If the astrological sign is the same for both, then that means that the two would be as similar as two peas in a pod.

My friend Gary from college was a real vagabond. He was one of those people who would just start talking to you as if you'd been friends all your lives. He became a true artist in the way he studied the ancient traditions and then he put the art into action. He could read a person's personality and life traits just by knowing their birth date and year. He was also a very smart guy, but he chose peace over prosperity. He found peace in replacing a broken water pipe or an electrical panel. He also loved boats and was perfectly happy taking care of them for rich people by living on them in exclusive neighborhoods, primarily in Florida. He always found time to just take off and travel around the United States looking up old friends. In 1977, he became Marisa's godfather. This had nothing to do with Chinese astrology, but was just a permanent link between him and Marisa. Gary used to pop in every five to ten years after college, but once the computer came on the scene, they began to communicate fairly often. Marisa was thrilled to learn Chinese Astrology, and Gary was more than happy to teach her. Marisa didn't take to it with the same intensity he did, and she didn't invest as much time in her studies, but she still became pretty good at a young age at reading people.

She has since learned that part of our plans when we are in spirit is to choose a birth date that will correspond with the type of human they want to be after our next birth. If someone decides they want to become a rock star and learn certain life lessons, for example, then they might choose to be born in the month of August, since that is the month when Leos are in the limelight. To have the strong ambition to succeed, this person may want to be born in the year of the rat, which is the first year of the twelve-year cycle. If a spirit wants to become a housewife with no other obligations beyond her family, she may want to be born in March and be a submissive person born early in the year of either the snake or the pig. These considerations are all parts of the planning process in Heaven. Before we choose the lives we want, we need to remember that everything can go haywire while we have our lifetime amnesia and having other family and societal influences. For the most part, there is hope that each spirit learns to find God through love and peace. We all need to find the Light within and put it to good use.

All religions have prayer traditions, but our guides have told us that God is a group consciousness of every one of His creations. His design of the universe includes a huge structure, or bureaucracy, as we think of it. We learned that the best way to describe God and how we are linked is to use an analogy just as Jesus used parables in his teaching. Marisa told me about a book she read that says we should think of God as a large ocean. All of God is in that water. A sea of water is taken from the ocean, and that is God's personality and human form and also His free will. That body of water is called Christ. God then put His first created soul, called the Holy Spirit, into Christ's water. The Holy Spirit is the knowledge of God and also the creator of all the angels whereas Christ is the creator of Souls.

The Holy Spirit is God's gift to Christ's creations and is a part of the water and cannot be separated. It is all one. Finding Christ through the recognition of Jesus is also discovering the Holy Spirit, but despite what the Bible says, you may find Christ without understanding the man Jesus. Believe me, the good Hindus and Muslims and Buddhists, et cetera, who haven't discovered Jesus are not destined for Hell. This is one of the reasons I am trying to get through to inquiring Christian minds like I used to have. I could sit in church and still not feel the Holy Spirit, whereas a righteous Buddhist could be at peace understanding who Christ is without referring to Christ as Christ but by some other name established long before Jesus appeared. In Hinduism, Christ's soul (Brahma's Soul) is the incarnated Krishna. Imagine that from the sea which contains the same water as the ocean come many different lakes of water (picture the Great Lakes). The water in each lake is still all the same water of God, Christ, and the Holy Spirit. It is still all God. Each of these lakes is called an Oversoul.[3]

---

[3] Christ gives off a piece of Himself to create the souls to run universes. He

God has free will, the Holy Spirit has free will, Christ has free will, and the Oversouls have free will while they are in charge of their lakes, or Super Universes. Our universe is one of many universes within our Star System or Super Universe, but it is home for our souls, whether in spirit or in human form. We occupy a very small spot in our Super Universe, or as the entities from above call it, our Star System. But as small as earth and its humans are in relation to everything God created, we are all still a part of Him. We are all the water, too.

Our Oversoul took little saucers of the water from the lakes, billions of them, and created Souls. Through the Soul, the Oversoul learns lessons that are then delivered through His consciousness to Christ so that Christ will grow, and then God would grow as well. Everything is transmitted through the Soul, or the water. Christ is the recipient and the deliverer of His free will to each piece of His creation. We are told that as human beings everything has to be explained in a linear fashion or a way we can understand. God's water is in Christ, which is really God's humanity and personality, and then through to the Oversouls and then through to each one of the Souls created by the Oversoul. You and I, each of us, are small energies or pieces of one of those billions of Souls created by Christ through the Oversoul. These individual Souls are a part of the group consciousness of the Oversoul, who is a member of the group consciousness of Christ, who is a group consciousness of God Himself.

From the Soul, the Higher Selves that eventually become you and me are then created when the Higher Self and the Soul

---

still calls them His children. The Oversouls then create innumerable Souls. From the Souls come what I call Lords, but others call these Souls the Higher Self. The writers, translators, and readers, and preachers of the Bible use the word Lord to describe whatever comes through from the other side, including God himself. From the Soul and the Higher Self/Lord come their pieces of themselves, or spirits. Yours and mine grow through experience through time and eventually merge with the level above us.

combine to create a spirit of themselves. This spirit is embedded into a human body by their choice.

Since I am Christian and since the word Lord is used very liberally throughout the Bible to refer to someone or something of a higher authority, as when the term is used to refer to the head of a household or applied to an angel in a dream or to God Himself. The Higher Self/Lord gives off a small part of His spirit to be incarnated in a human body, or vessel, as they call it. When that spirit, that portion of the Higher Self or Lord as we Christians refer to Him, comes to inhabit the human body, it comes with amnesia. That spirit, that creation by our Soul through our Higher Self, which is you or me, I, is plunked down into a savage human body on an earth that is influenced by Lucifer (I'll get into that shortly) and, to top it off, with amnesia and not a clue that we were once living souls in Heaven. Thinking in a linear fashion, depending upon how many times we have incarnated in human bodies, determines the level of growth of our Higher Self, which, again, is me and you. Initially, the greatest level to get to is the seventh, where the Spirit of Jesus resides and where the souls of the likes of Noah and Moses reside in council as part of the group consciousness of Jesus. To get any farther than Level Seven of our universe (there are more levels of seven levels above us), to reach the Right Hand of God, means having to join the group consciousness of our Higher Self; and then the group consciousness of our Soul, and then the group consciousness of our Oversoul, and then through our creator, Christ (for Christians, please see John 14:6). In the following example, I'll try my best to explain what a group consciousness is.

This may be simplistic, but think of God as the developer of a large, worldwide company like McDonalds, with Christ as the CEO. In today's world, there is no Mr. McDonald. McDonalds is a collective of the thoughts, the energy, of its original founder. The original founder really was a Mr. McDonald, but one day a Mr. Ray Kroc stopped into this little San Bernardino hamburger joint that only sold hamburgers, fries, and shakes. Ray Kroc thought that it was simple enough to franchise, so he bought Mr. McDonald's hamburger joint and kept the name.

Next, Mr. Kroc established a plan. One of the first things he did was to hire people who thought very much like he did. Think of his first employees as clones with free will. He put them in positions of importance as decision makers, that is, the board of directors.

The first Mr. McDonald was not God. But there was a knowledge that was created in the mind of the first Mr. McDonald to create the simple plan in the first place. We can call that created "idea" or "plan," which was only for success and for good, the Holy Spirit. The Holy Spirit is the knowledge of God. The Holy Spirit is the knowledge and fortitude of the plan simply known as McDonalds. (And this Holy Spirit also reserves the ability to create pieces of itself to become the company trainers, the employees of the corporation that can help every employee from time to time with their work).

So Mr. Kroc has now surrounded himself with people who are basically Mr. Kroc clones but have free will, too. They begin to expand into many stores around the world. Each member of the board of directors takes on a different continent to be in charge of. They, too, have the ability to make clones of themselves, or franchisees who will now be clones of clones of Mr. Kroc, God. They each have the spirit of Mr. Kroc. Each McDonald's store, of course, will be headed up by a manager who is now a clone of the franchisee.

Everyone knows the plan. But business is going crazy, so now all those cooks and counter people who are clones of the manager are being promoted to store managers, and the cloned managers start overseeing new stores. "McDonalds" (God) continues to grow and experience something new every day. Everyone who belongs to the organization is a product of the Holy Spirit or God or the idea, "McDonalds," and the spirit of Mr. Kroc (God). As the employees progress up the organization and take on more responsibility, they, too, hire people who want

85

to learn the idea and the plan. These people are pieces of the energy (more clones) of the employer who hires each new person because these people are people the boss thinks will think like him and work for the common good of the idea, McDonalds.

Now McDonalds has a core that runs the organization and as the organization grows, so does the number or people in the innermost operations, or core, of McDonalds. There are now regional management offices with regional boards of directors. The combined group, all the regional, national, and international district managers, is the combined consciousness of the organization that, instead of calling it the group consciousness of McDonalds, we'll call the group consciousness of God. God is McDonalds (and each and every employee is a piece, through cloning, of Mr. Kroc, Christ). God is a group consciousness of the core of those who stand at the top of an organization and wield the plans. They have graduated from the lowest levels to the top and now sit at the right hand of Mr. Kroc. These clones, we'll call Souls/Spirits, keep graduating up the ranks in Heaven.

Now there are millions of McDonald's stores and there are almost as many franchise owners. Each store is filled with the lowest level employees, but they, too, are parts of the group, or group consciousness, of McDonalds. These are Level One employees. Those who run the organization at the highest level, we call Level Sevens. That is where Mr. Kroc (Christ) sits.

Everyone is human, with mind, body, ego, and spirit, and everyone, including Mr. Kroc (Christ) who decided to add cheeseburgers to the original plan, has free will. But in our world, the lowest levels, the Ones and Twos, are the most likely to be prone to errors of judgment. Sometimes error happens because they just don't know any better and haven't quite figured out Mr. McDonald's (God's) plan. Level Ones are people who have never worked before. They have no experience. But if they listen and see the attitude, professionalism, and the light of the employee just above them, and others around them, too, that are happy and peaceful, then maybe they'll come to feel like they're the spirit of the organization, too. They learn the plan and thus know McDonalds (God) and that he, the organization, has a plan for the good of all. Not just for the employees, but for all the customers (society), too.

The first part of the plan, the most basic part of the plan, is to have the Level One and up employees go home in peace every day after work. The environment at work should be filled with positive energy, but we all know that sometimes there is someone who, as we call it, is the rotten apple that spoils the barrel, the person that somehow comes to work there, too. The manager thinks he sees the light in this new applicant, but he has made an error in judgment. His free will (using his ego and mind) hired someone of questionable ability to become part of the plan. But this person is someone whose idea is to use his ego and mind to do dark things like rob, steal, cheat, and basically take advantage of the Light nature of those around him. This person is a Level One who is influenced by a different plan, which is to get ahead of everyone else in whatever way it takes to do it. He doesn't care what effect his ambition has on any of the other employees, or even on his manager. His plan is the antithesis of the plan of McDonalds, which we called the Holy Spirit, which, again, is the knowledge of the plan and knowing McDonalds and what McDonalds stands for.

The idea that this ambitious young man has is called Satanism. It was created out of the free will of one of those boards of directors. That director's name is Mr. Lucifer. His "Holy Spirit" or the knowledge of his plan is called Satanism. This is the name that Mr. Lucifer uses to identify his idea. Satanism is the permeating knowledge of Mr. Lucifer's plan. It is in direct battle with the Holy Spirit. Satanism is the antithesis of McDonald's plan. Satan has a plan to deceive and someday become Mr. McDonald and to eliminate the knowledge of the original plan, the Holy Spirit. Darkness is the vehicle. Darkness doesn't see the Light of the plan of McDonalds (the Holy Spirit), but wishes to defeat, or at least injure, as many of the lower level employees, the Level Ones, that he can corrupt so that he can destroy McDonalds.

The employee that has Satan's plan thinks those who follow the manual, the Level Twos who are trying to improve themselves and get to know McDonalds and what it stands for through the study of the manual, are easy pickings to fool and teach the ways of the darkness. Sometimes this employee can infiltrate the thinking of many levels above him, too, and he does try. But his easiest marks are people at the first and second level.

Second level people really want to learn the idea of McDonalds and rise to the top, right into the innermost circle where the give and take of the board of directors, who devise everything for the good of McDonalds stand together in one thought. So these second level people take their corporate McDonald's manuals (their Bibles) and study and study and study. They are faithful to the book that was presented to them that gives them a path to the highest positions through special knowledge. These people really try hard to learn. But, doggone it; they're still working for minimum wage! That sneaky fellow who could care less about the manual (Bible) is pocketing some of the cash register without ringing up the sales, and he's got more money than anyone else. And, he's got a nice car. Your second level mind is thinking, *I really need a lot of money to help my mother who is ill and that is a very noble reason to want money. But it says, in the book, not to steal from the company or you will be fired and go to jail (a jail with fire), because the book says they can call the police.* You are so torn. You trust the book, and you know what is right. But there is that temptation. That sneaky guy just smiles at you and flaunts his wares. He gets away with it somehow.

Sometimes some of those higher-ups, like the third, fourth, or even fifth level employees are tempted to embezzle some of all that daily cash that comes along, but this is very rare. Sometimes these people are like Mr. Thieving Level One when they are hired, but they are able to deceive everyone along the path of promotion and hide their belief in Mr. Lucifer's idea; the idea of Satanism. These wayward souls were heavily influenced by the dark idea, Satan's idea, to do something that actually harms McDonalds (God). The creator of the Satanic thought is Mr. Lucifer, who is now a very powerful member of the board of directors, too. Fortunately, his district is not the entire world, but just his assigned portion of it. And for all the most successful of the employees within that area, such as Mr. Stalin, Mr. Hitler, and Mr. Pol Pot, these men have graduated to being the purest of the dark side's Holy Spirit. They have now become more influential in the plan of Mr. Lucifer and sit at his right hand and remain very far away from the light of McDonalds. Mr. Lucifer is still on the board of directors of McDonalds because he thinks what he is doing is what is best for McDonalds. His free will has become so distorted by the standards of the light, of the real idea of McDonalds, that in his mind, in his free will, he thinks he knows what is best for McDonalds. Along with his own circle or board of directors, his goal is to overtake the entire board of directors of McDonalds and rule McDonalds by his plan of Satanism.

The foregoing is an example of how God, through the guides and the angels, have been telling us what the universe and what God is all about. I'm trying to say, in this example that God started out at one point as an energy that had a plan. The knowledge of the plan was simply the Holy Spirit. But someone had to implement the plan, and that was Christ. Christ became Mr. Kroc and began to expand his energy to create new souls that would follow the plan he was assigned to carry out. He was creating, using pieces of his own energy, to create, basically clones of himself. These clones are Souls. The Souls then know the plan, but have free will. They know the plan, they see the light, and the light is the plan.

You and I were created a long time ago. Some might say that God is an evolutionist of sorts. God is eternal. There was never *nothing* because *even nothing is something*. God created Himself in spirit and personality as Christ and man and (the female aspect of Himself) as the Holy Spirit. The guides broke in with:

Eden: "We would like to share with you that every soul has the polarity of male and feminine. Take that out, or that every living thing has the masculine and feminine energies. In a future time, and possibly another place, a single sense of self can happen, but at this time, no; all souls carry the duality of feminine and masculine and therefore human spirits do, too."

But in order to create life and then, eventually, humans, He needed to create constellations and galaxies and solar systems and planets. Each inhabited planet was designed in a fashion as to create an environment for life. God could have blinked His eyes and created the perfect worlds, but each layer of His administration had free will input. Therefore, planets and solar systems and galaxies and constellations were all designed differently, but yet with the same purpose. The purpose was for God to recreate Himself into human form. But first He needed to create the building blocks of humanity in order for souls, spirits, you and me, to have vessels to live in. Just to make things a hair more complicated, God created these worlds for *all* mammals to have souls. Mammals would have souls that would evolve until such time that they would graduate to become human souls.

Think of our earth. It took a long time to create in our terms of time. To God, there is no time. They keep telling us this in these taped conversations, but it is pretty hard to wrap my mind around such a concept because time is all we know. Nevertheless, over time, conditions became substantive enough to create life on earth. Christ, with our Oversoul, became the creators and designers of our universe and thus, their earth. When it came time for humans, the Holy Spirit, who also creates the angels in addition to residing in every soul, went to work. (Angels never become humans yet are created with the specific job to assist humans.)[4]

---

[4] Eden: "The angels wish to attain the status of archangel as souls aspire to become ascended master. Think of Moses as an ascended master working in council with Christ."

The angels are able to make their selves visible at times just as Paul wrote in the New Testament (I paraphrase), *"Be careful how you treat a stranger for that stranger could be an angel."* I say that because the angels, working in conjunction with ascended human spirits that had once resided on other earthlike planets, created all life on earth. At various stages throughout the evolution of our planet, these angels came to earth like scientists and creatively worked with the evolutionary patterns of all living things. What God did was create souls for all mammals. One of our big surprises is to go to Heaven and see all forms of mammals there, even those that are now extinct. Each mammal evolves and gets closer to finding God. Most of it is strictly instinctive. Most mammals just know God exists. They understand their own environment and therefore learn to coexist within their environment with mammals of their own design as well as with the different forms of mammals around them. These non-human mammals also live by the human credo of *Fight or Flight* as well, but they don't have governments and laws to know how to get along. That's what it is like in "Heaven." Up there, there is just love and everyone getting along. Not like on earth, where a lion is about to pounce on one of those peaceful mammals.

Lower mammals can eventually evolve spiritually to become a new human spirit under the guidance of the Lord and the full administration above it. You and I were each, at one time in the evolution of the earth, a mammal of some kind. That is why sometimes people will swear they remember being a wolf or a whale. They think that is crazy and only true in their stupid dreams when in reality, that is what we all were at one time. Eventually, we graduate to becoming the spirits that we are today. Plant souls evolve to become reptilian souls who become mammal souls who evolve to become human souls. The process never goes backward. We are forever evolving into the group consciousness of the level above us.

In referring to levels, there are levels within levels within levels within levels. There is so much to learn and experience.

91

We may live as a woman and then next live as a man. There is constant balance in the universe. We can call it the yin and yang, positive and negative, black and white. Live as a pauper, and then live as a lord among men. These are all the experiences we design for ourselves.

Gary obviously designed himself to be a vagabond to find his peace. What God is and always will be is Peace and Love. That is our greatest goal in this human life and that is to live in peace and love with our neighbor. It is our human mind and ego that gets in the way of finding that peace and love. Jesus had reduced all the dos and don'ts in the Old Testament down to loving your neighbor as yourself and loving God with all your heart and soul. These are our divine rules. But we have amnesia. Only trusting in the Lord, in the Soul, in Christ, and the Holy Spirit, are we able to find the path we have set for ourselves.

Sometimes we will design grief and hard times into our lives. This is done in conjunction with our Soul Group and Soul Family. Experiencing grief is just part of human life. Even the higher mammals experience the grief of lost loved ones. God gave us the Holy Spirit so that knowing God will allow us to continue to have faith when grief and tragedy strike. In one life, you may design yourself to be a child that will die unexpectedly, and then in the next life will be as a parent that loses a child. These lives are designed for us to learn lessons. That is why trusting God, our Lord, when tragedy strikes is good because, as we humans put it, the Lord has our back. He will comfort us.

Our angels told us to talk to God as if He were sitting right there in the chair next to you because, in reality, He really is right there next to you. You just can't see Him. They said that prayer is very important because it is our way of telling every level above us that we put our absolute trust in each of them to help us carry out our individual plans, even when grief strikes. Every single spirit and, thus, human being is best to learn how to turn the Light of Christ on every day. They said that by giving over our individual free will to God, we are turning on the power of the universe. We are giving permission to our entire lineage to help us to stay on track so that we can learn the lessons we came here for despite being amnesiacs.

When Gary was nearing the end of his life at the age of sixty-eight, he went home to Michigan to be around his children. His oldest child, Chris, took care of him in his home. Gary loved his Chinese astrology, but he never connected it with God. Marisa decided that with her newfound love of the Lord and in Christ, she should try to prepare Gary for what was to come when he went "home." Gary was hard to convince, but between Marisa and me, we at least had him convinced enough that he wasn't merely going to go into a box and that would be the end of him. Chris was agnostic bordering on being an atheist. He believed that we were meant to be good persons to our fellow men, but he believed this is all there is. Just prior to Gary's passing, he and his son, Chris, would get into knock-down arguments about who we are, why we are, and whether we are going any further beyond this life. So to keep peace in the household, they decided to use a word that once uttered meant the conversation/argument would come to an abrupt end. That word was "purple." Neither Marisa nor I had any knowledge of this prior to Gary's passing.

When Gary passed away in the summer of 2012, Marisa was distraught. She knew where he was going and only hoped she would be able to communicate with him once he got to the other side. By now, Marisa was bringing a lot of skeptics to becoming lovers of Christ and God. By word of mouth, people were flocking to Marisa because she was able to see through charades or through actual telepathy and communicate with members of a grieving person's family or friend who had passed away. These departed spirits would convey messages to Marisa that only the grieving person would know. Much like what my own dad conveyed to me in my first Reiki session with Marisa.

Through her early life experiences, Marisa was unfortunate enough to see people close to her, and so young, die. Jason, probably the biggest influence of ways of the darkness to Marisa, was one who died of an overdose. Marisa was distraught when he passed, even though she had long ended the relationship they once had. But when Gary died, her sense of loss was dramatic. She was depressed because she started to doubt her God-given abilities. Then, while we were doing a tape-recorded conversation, a spirit came in hopping around on a pogo stick waving a piece of purple paper. Marisa was upset that Gary wasn't speaking to her, but she was glad to see that he looked happy. He was young again, with no illness at all, and he was hopping around on a pogo stick waving a purple piece of paper.

Chris had contacted us through email, thanking us for sending the flowers for Gary's funeral. I had never met or spoken to Chris, but after this session of seeing Gary (Marisa did, not me), I thought I would give him a call and let Chris know what we experienced. At first our conversation was light with memories of Gary and his life. Chris wasn't especially proud of his dad since Gary never really amounted to a whole lot in this crazy secular world we live in. Because of the vagabond life that Gary had lived, Chris thought that if there was a Heaven and Hell, surely Gary was going to Hell. But Chris made it clear that he believed there was no God and that this life is what it is because we evolved from apes. We are only a part of the earth and no more, and when we die, we die. We're done, over. Chris began getting a little heated in our conversation while I was trying to convince him otherwise, that God is very real and Heaven is our reality, not this world. He thought I was crazy to waste time praying to God. I told him that we had experienced Gary from the other side. I told him that Gary was hopping around on a pogo stick vigorously waving a purple piece of paper. When I asked him if there was any significance to a pogo stick or a purple piece of paper, he paused for a very long time and then, when he spoke, it was as if I were speaking to another person. Chris had begun to weep. He said that his crazy dad used to love pogo sticks, and then he told me the significance of the word "purple."

Chris learned, through Marisa's abilities to see Gary on the other side, that God was real after all. Nobody knew the significance of the word *purple* but Chris and Gary. Chris finally realized that Gary truly had moved on. His dad wasn't just in a box but had returned "home" to his old consciousness prior to being incarnated as Gary. He is now the same spirit he was when he lived different human lives before. Therefore, Gary is now part of the group consciousness of all of his previous lives, including his latest.   Here is what "they" said in further explanation after we read this section to them for clarification.

Eden, regarding group consciousness: "To simplify, use the example of Gary returning to the consciousness, or the remaining energy of his Spirit that allows him to remember all his past lives and therefore all the Gary's together now make up the newest Gary, a Gary that experienced life again and hopefully learned new lessons or completed lessons he was unable to complete or conquer in a previous life, but now remembers all those past lives....his group consciousness."

We learned some basics in these two taped conversations. From there, we proceeded to have thirty-plus hours of further conversations with our angels and guides as well as all sorts of ascended former humans. From there, we were able to ask further questions in return for further clarifications.

Boxes

(I have received quite a few comments about this chapter by those who have read rough manuscripts of this book and given us their opinions and comments, for which I am most grateful. This chapter is in here because I, Joe Moris, am trying to make a point. Furthermore, this book is meant to be light and avoid all negativity or darkness whenever possible. But just as there are yin and yang, balance, I'm going out on a limb here because I think it is important to say, as a Christian who is new to all of this, that we religious types essentially stick ourselves into boxes. Therefore, in this section, which is not long, I am an equal-opportunity offender to our institutionalized religions. I will stick only to the four main religions: Judaism, Islam, Hinduism, and Christianity.[5] There is some wisdom from above in this chapter, but it is mostly my understanding of the religions and not instruction from the other side. So please don't judge the whole book by this one chapter.)

We don't end our life in a box. We move on. We go home. We go back to where we started. We go home to be ourselves again. We just change dimensions. We go home to the group consciousness of ourselves and our previous lives. We go home and remember who we were before we lived our most recent lives experiencing the human condition. I have had many lives and have learned many life lessons. Sometimes I learned the lessons I came to earth to learn, but sometimes I wasn't successful.

Again, we come with amnesia, and that is the plan. Even Jesus didn't know He was spirit until He was baptized by John and confronted by His Father in the Jordan River. It was after

---

[5] Buddhism is a philosophy of learning to find wisdom. Buddhism does not have a god per se, but teaches that we are to love as it is done in all the other dimensions. Surely there will be a bit more about Buddhism in our next book, which will go further into the design of Heaven and the dimensions as well as the physical universe we live in.

that baptism that Jesus had all the profound understanding of His real self, Christ. Jesus came directly as the perfect personification of Christ. I understood from the conversations that Jesus did not come through the Oversoul or a Soul or a Higher Self but that he came directly from Christ. But we've also been told that Jesus was "Christed," which means He earned His way to becoming the owner and operator of our universe. This should be explained much further in our next book, when we describe the universe and the dimensions.

Prior to being born as a boy named Yeshua, Christ sat with all the ascended masters and the archangels, including Gabriel, and planned His life as a human. The angels and those who had already been Christed, the ascended masters, would be around Him (invisibly) at all times during His time on the earth. When Jesus prayed to the Father, He was praying to the entire group consciousness of God and the Holy Spirit. That is why Jesus was so protective of the Holy Spirit in His teachings.

A seed of His greatness was planted in His human mind and ego by His mother after she was visited by the Archangel Gabriel. Jesus was the perfect manifestation of Christ in human form. Jesus was God in His perfection. Even though Jesus had free will, He was perfect in following the Father and freely gave of His spirit and free will in favor of God's will at all times. Even knowing who He was, Jesus was still human and was found reciting the Twenty-Second Psalm at His crucifixion, asking God "Why would you forsake me?"

Now if even Jesus had lingering feelings of humanity, you know our human road is a tough one because none of us are the perfect manifestation of Christ. In our condition of amnesia, life on earth is all we know. God, Christ, our Oversoul, our Soul, and our Higher Self (cumulatively, the "Lord") all have a stake in our development. Fortunately or unfortunately, we have free will, which can easily tune out our spirit, our Higher Self, or (as it is frequently called by those in the Bible) our Lord. Our guides also pointed out:

Christed: Those who have been Christed are assigned their own universes. Created by Christ and the Holy Spirit, many souls have worked their way through each of the many levels necessary to become like Christ in every way. The soul that was Jesus Christ learned and grew through time and incarnated as one of each of His higher creations to become Christed. This is where all the knowledge was stored in this young boy, Yeshua (Jesus). The "Soul" or "Spirit" of Jesus knew it was God.

Christ had incarnated on earth at least two times before coming as Jesus. The first time may have been as Krishna, and then He came later as Melchizedek. Krishna taught His followers about the reality of the *Trimurti* (three heads on one neck, often facing different directions), which became the Christian Trinity of Father, Son, and Holy Spirit. God was Brahma, Shiva was the Holy Spirit, and Vishnu was the Son. Krishna was Vishnu incarnated. The Hindu religion has come to accept that Jesus, too, was the Soul of Vishnu.

Later, as Melchizedek, Christ sat with Abraham and convinced the patriarch (whose name at that time was Abram) of the one and only God and the concept of the Trinity. Abraham lived at a time when there were many perceived gods that were followed by people who were later called gentiles. Abraham was the father of the Hebrew religion, which eventually led to the coming of Christ in Jesus and the subsequent Christian religion.[6]

---

[6] Jeremy said that Abraham is an ascended master. Our second book will have the anatomy of the soul, the creation, and will include some scintillating answers to some of the earth's mysteries. A second guide, who never appeared but communicated by talking, has asked us to have the book be strictly a channeled book. They like the pure teachings they are bringing to us. They say that if we bring in other teachings, people will be confused. They told us in the beginning of this book not to bring in knowledge from other books or opinions. They said that although some may be accurate, a lot can be addressed later in another book, where there will be more depth in discussions of the structure of the soul and the universe.

Islam was founded about 600 years after the death of Jesus and about 300 years after the Bible was copied and distributed by Roman Emperor Constantine. Just as Jesus' mother Mary was visited by the Archangel Gabriel, so too were Elizabeth, the mother of John the Baptist and Aminah bint Wahb, the mother of Mohammad. Being visited by the Archangel Gabriel is a big deal:

Eden: Gabriel has never been human. Angels are not human and are not Souls. They are messengers of God. These are all high vibrating souls, including Mary and Joseph and Mary's kinswoman (possibly her cousin) Elizabeth, who bore John the Baptist. Angels aspire to reach the status of Gabriel as souls aspire to be Christed, to be like Christ. Angels may also be "temporary" humans when that is the only way to assist the soul they materialized as human for. (Joe: What this means is that angels may be given permission to take on a human body temporarily in order to appear to someone. That is what happened in the book of Isaiah. Isaiah had a hard time communicating and seeing the other side. Therefore, the "lord" was an angel of God who took human form in order to speak directly to Isaiah, to give Isaiah prophesy. Paul wrote in Corinthians that you should be careful when meeting a stranger for "you may be in the presence of an angel".

Mohammad was to be a teacher and healer, as were Jesus and John. Islam, when memorialized, became a religion with Mohammad's writing of the Koran (or Qur'an). Mohammad was not only a deliverer of the knowledge of God, but his human ego, mind, and body was also a secular warrior. Mohammad was a brave leader and a brave warrior for Allah. He was led to believe and to sermonize that those who did not believe in Allah and live by His word, what he alone believed were God's commands, were therefore enemies (infidels) of Allah and deserved death. Again, this was the seventh century, and society wasn't exactly as savvy as we are today because time does bring wisdom, if nothing else.

Unfortunately, though, Islam has caused a great rift in the world today. It is not like the inclusive religion of Hinduism and Buddhism. Followers of Mohammad continue to believe that if you do not follow Islam, you are considered an infidel and are thus an enemy of God, who they call Allah. Unfortunately the most militant in their religion think they are perfectly justified sending you "home." They think they are doing God's work and feel that they will be awarded in Paradise (Heaven). Our Heavenly teachers have been clear that we are judged by intent. A person who defends himself and kills another does not do so with malicious intent. The soul of a human that takes the life of another with the intent that he or she can blame or award God for their action will have a big price to pay in their review when they go "home." It won't be a pretty picture, because there really is a Hell. Muslims, too, love their neighbor, even as Jesus professes. It is only that very small percentage like the Al Qaeda terrorists that give Islam a bad name in the world today.

The peaceful religion of Hinduism has become inclusive of other religions, including Buddhism and Christianity. In my own experience and travels, though, there is some tension between Hindus and Muslims because Hindus will never bow to killing other humans in the name of God or Brahma. Hindus believe that God is everything, which is true. In my opinion, Hindus believe that a plant or a tree or a cow is on equal footing with a human being because everything is precious in the eyes of God. I also believe that Hindus may be the closest to understanding what we are presenting in this book. They believe in reincarnation, but they also believe that a person who fails in this human life could be reincarnated as something other than a human. The earth was designed to have humans at the top of the food chain and suitable for inhabitation by the soul. Therefore, a Hindu who feels he has broken the rules of God or society lives in his own Hell and believes that his next incarnation may be as a monkey or a frog. According to our teachers, that is not possible.

A soul will never go backwards. The soul will always grow forward and incarnate as human to learn human lessons.

Jews, too, have transformed their religion from all the rules found in the Torah (the first five books of the Old Testament) into a religion now devoid of Christ's simple teaching *to love one another as yourself and to love God with all your heart and soul*. Jesus was recognized by the early Christian church as a teacher sent by God, but right up to today, the Jews are still waiting for the Messiah who rides a mighty horse and carries a sword and, like David, will become a ruler among men on earth. Judaism is a religion of customs and earthly rules. Personally, I have worked with many people who call themselves Jewish, but I did not know one who went to Temple on Saturday. It could be my own small sample, but I find that Jews just don't want the guilt associated with all the rules found in the first five books of the Bible, and therefore just call themselves Jewish and avoid religion entirely. In fact, many Jews I've come to know speak very well of Jesus Christ. They just don't believe he is God.

Even Christianity has splintered into varying convolutions of the Word. In Ireland, for example, even though they have somewhat different interpretations of the Bible, Protestants and Catholics still murder each other. Islam, too, has been convoluted in many respects to where the radicals of Islam still follow the fierce rules as laid out by Mohammad. Abraham had two sons, one (Ishmael) from his concubine, Hagar, the other (Isaac) from his wife, Sarah. Those two sons are said to have founded two separate philosophies that eventually became religions (Islam from Ishmael, Judaism from Isaac). Rules and laws keep society civil and are important. Rules keep society intact, but that doesn't stop Sunnis from murdering Shiites in the Muslim world any more than Christian leaders keep Protestants from killing Catholics and vice versa.

God has rules, too. These are Light, Love, and Spirit. Without them, His universal organization couldn't stay intact. But just like in the lower realms of human society, heavenly rules have been broken. One of the oldest and brightest of Souls at one time was Lucifer. But he decided not to follow God's rules. He has since created a dimension of his own, which is bent on acquiring as many of God's spirits as he can. Where these spirits live is what we call Hell.

Eden: "Lucifer created his own rules. God gives all His beings free will. God does not set rules. He is Light and Spirit and Unconditional Love. God only conveys the representation of truth, but all His creations have free will. Souls are carried back to this Light. Lucifer didn't choose to not follow God's rules, but chose to create his own rules. Saying Lucifer went against God is not accurate. God does not set rules, and all souls are given free will. The Light of God is the beacon to which all souls are drawn. Lucifer chose to turn away from the Light and create his own version of Heaven. He thought that since life is eternal anyway, he would choose another direction for his soul to experience." [Transcribed from the tape].

Religions have become boxes that humans have accepted, only to create their own Hells. All religions have their "don'ts." When we don't do what our religion tells us to do, if we break any of the "rules," then we doom ourselves to Hell in our own minds. When we are doomed to Hell in our minds, then it is easy to lose the Light that Christ has given us in Him through the Holy Spirit. God is Love. God is Peace. God is Light. If someone drifts away from Christ's light and feels that they have no chance with God's favor, they then tend to ignore Him and go through life feeding off their pride and ego. This does much damage that is harmful to their spirit, their Soul. When they lose the Light and their spirit, they're giving their soul to the dark side. Then their spirit will experience Hell.

Hell is real. It's where Satan and Lucifer rule. As I understand it, Lucifer was a bright Soul that decided that he did not want to become a part of the group Consciousness of Christ and thus became an enemy of Christ. He, too, is a Soul, a very high-standing Soul, but he has not been Christed. Unfortunately, the Soul of Lucifer resides and rules this little part of our universe. As in my McDonalds example, Lucifer is merely a franchisee of one of the McDonalds. He is cornered in this part of the universe, and earth is one of his domains. Therefore, Satan and his lord, Lucifer, are always at work.

Christ would not allow Lucifer's *created* spirits to live on earth after Jesus came and took possession of earth as the Son of Man; therefore, Lucifer still controls Hell, and earth remains his playground in defiance of Christ. He wants as many of Christ's spirits as he can get and will use whatever means necessary to get them. Since we have amnesia and forgot that we were spirit before we were humans, and because earth lies in the domain of Lucifer, we humans have an uphill battle trying to find God and Christ, who are our portals through the darkness that Lucifer spreads. God created the magnificence of earth, but Lucifer was given domain over it prior to the arrival of Adam and Eve and ruled it prior to the coming of Christ in Jesus. He no longer controls earth, but he is still in possession of it, along with the fallen spirits that roam the earth, sometimes in human disguise.

Since I call myself a Christian, it is hard for me to think that I am in a box. I want to learn everything I can, but I am also obsessed with wanting to make sure that our conversations are not with Lucifer and the dark side. Every good Christian gives me that raised eyebrow when I tell them what I am experiencing, but the dicta of the Bible leave them concerned for my spiritual soul. But I have become convinced now that Marisa and I are not being influenced by evil. As Jesus said, a house divided cannot stand. If Lucifer and Satan are at war with God, then why would they be glorifying God to us? Why would they revere Christ the way they do if they don't like God? By doing so, they are a house divided and thus cannot stand.

I believe that lords have visited this earth many times at the request of the prophets and others. In a modern way, that is what is happening with Marisa. She has been given a gift of energy that allows her to freely enter a realm, the astral realm, the next step above earth. It is a step below where we started, an in-between place, where everyone goes first to go through a proper transition from amnesia back to reality. But if the spirits, souls, guides, angels, and other heavenly friends above us want to communicate with the likes of Marisa as they did with the prophets in the Bible and as they did with the apostles of Jesus, then they are able to lower their energy levels enough to meet Marisa in an in-between place called the astral realm.

The Bible

Whenever Marisa's abilities are brought to the attention of the clergy we have discussed this book with, we receive looks that are a combination of fear and pity. The Bible has made it clear to those of the cloth that the use of mediums and spiritists is strictly forbidden. They use verses given in Leviticus and Deuteronomy:

Leviticus 19:31: *Do not turn to mediums or spiritists; do not seek them out to be defiled by them.*

Leviticus 20:27: *Now a man or a woman who is a medium or a spiritist shall surely be put to death. They shall be stoned with stones....*

Yet Leviticus 20:26-28 also states:

26: You shall not eat anything with the blood, nor practice divination or soothsaying.

27: You shall not round off the side growth of your heads nor harm the edges of your beards.

28: You shall not make any cuts in your body for the dead nor make any tattoo marks on yourselves.

Leviticus 20:9-20 lists a series of sins:

9: If there is anyone who curses his father or his mother, he shall surely be put to death;

10: If there is a man who commits adultery with another man's wife, one who commits adultery with his friend's wife, the adulterer and the adulteress shall surely be put to death.

12: If there is a man who lies with a male as those who lie with a woman, both of them have committed a detestable act; they shall surely be put to death.

18: If there is a man who lies with a menstruous woman and uncovers her nakedness, he has laid bare her flow, and she has exposed the flow of her blood; thus both of them shall be cut off from among their people.

These are just a few examples of the "don'ts" given in a small part of the Book of Leviticus, which is a lengthy dialogue between Moses and God. The Jews were a beaten lot who had just experienced 600 years of enslavement. God brought Moses to them to take them out of their misery and into a land of their own. God laid down some very stringent rules to turn the Jews, over the course of forty years, into a submissive people and to weed out impurities in their ranks. This Old Testament God might be considered a cruel god, but He also presented miracle after miracle to keep His people alive in the desert. But he was making it clear that there was only one god and that He was that God, and He was to be respected and worshipped.

As I read Leviticus, I said to myself, *Okay, I'm dead because I remember times that I cursed my parents for, well, being parents.* According to Leviticus, my friends with tattoos who are faithful followers of Christ would be cut off from God. Those acquaintances of mine that have been dealing with the inner turmoil of homosexuality would be stoned to death, and when I was in college, almost every guy had a beard, and we trimmed them to at least be somewhat presentable. That would be enough to throw me into a wilderness and be cut off from everyone.

Dealing with mediums and spiritists is one of those rules, and today's pastors still look at that rule and condemn someone like Marisa. When Marisa began to seek out God, she wanted to communicate directly with God and to see His face. I think most everyone would like to have that ability, but the angels said we would instantly die if we saw the face of God. The energy is too great for us to withstand. Moses was fortunate, as was Jesus, but so, too, were the prophets and disciples in the Bible. They were all able to seek out their Lord and hear or see Him while awake or in dreams. Marisa was given a gift from God to speak directly with angels and at times with souls that have passed on.

They interrupted me to say that Marisa has been given the ability to "speak to the heavenly realms." Apparently, this is more than just angels and loved ones who have passed. There are many universes and many dimensions, and Marisa has the ability to tap into visitors from everywhere in the "heavenly realms," including the astral and etheric planes.

Pastors also cite passages from the Book of Samuel where Saul, who is facing certain defeat before the Philistines and the loss of his kingship to David, in a last ditch effort to find out some prophesy to defeat the Philistines, goes to a medium. He needed to speak with the greatly beloved king Samuel, who had died.

Now, prior to this, Saul had banished all the mediums, spiritists, prophets, and prophetesses from his kingdom. So when he sought out a spiritess, the spiritess, not knowing that he was Saul, told him she was not allowed to give him prophesy by the king's rule. Saul told her (1Samuel: 28) that he would not kill her. Earlier in the book of Samuel, David had slain Goliath, and the people loved David. They sang songs about how Saul had killed thousands of the enemy, but that David had killed tens of thousands of the enemy. Saul was bitter and did not like being compared to David. He wanted David eliminated. Saul sensed that his people were tired of him and his viciousness and intention to eliminate anyone who challenged his authority. He was determined to not only eliminate the Philistines, but David, too, and thus he went to the spiritess for help.

David, who is revered throughout the Old Testament and is part of the bloodline that flows directly to Jesus, was told by the prophet Gad to go out of the stronghold and land of the Moabites, who were protecting him from Saul, and go into the land of Judah. Again, here is a case where the Bible refers to someone with an ability to speak to God, the prophet Gad, and yet when someone who is not of high recognition within the hierarchy of the Jews does the same thing, they are considered a medium or spiritist. To me, that is very confusing. Here is how the story is presented in Samuel 28:1-23:

1. Now it came about in those days that the Philistines gathered their armed camps for war, to fight against Israel. And Achish said to David: "Know assuredly that you will go out with me in the camp, you and your men."

2. David said to Achish, "Very well, you shall know what your servant can do." So Achish said to David, "Very well, I will make you my bodyguard for life."

3. Now Samuel was dead, and all Israel had lamented him and buried him in Ramah, his own city. And Saul had removed from the land those who were mediums and spiritists.

4. So the Philistines gathered together and came and camped in Shunem; and Saul gathered all Israel together and they camped in Gilboa.

5. When Saul saw the camp of the Philistines, he was afraid and his heart trembled greatly.

6. When Saul inquired of the LORD, the Lord did not answer him, either by dreams or by Urim (a council of God in Heaven made up of Judges and Archangels) or by prophets.

7. Then Saul said to his servants, "Seek for me a woman who is a medium that I may go to her and inquire of her." And his servants said to him, "Behold, there is a woman who is a medium at En-dor."

8. Then Saul disguised himself by putting on other clothes, and went, he and two men with him, and they came to the woman by night; and he said, "Conjure up for me, please, and bring up for me whom I shall name to you."

9. But the woman said to him, "Behold, you know what Saul has done, how he has cut off those who are mediums and spiritists from the land. Why are you then laying a snare for my life to bring about my death?" Saul vowed to her by the LORD, saying, "As the LORD lives, no punishment shall come upon you for this thing."

10. Then the woman said, "Whom shall I bring up for you?" and he said, "Bring up Samuel for me." When the woman saw Samuel, she cried out with a loud voice; and the woman spoke to Saul saying; "Why have you deceived me? For you are Saul."

11. The king said to her, "Do not be afraid; but what do you see?" And the woman said to Saul, "I see a divine being coming up out of the earth."

12. He said to her, "What is his form?" And she said, "An old man is coming up and he is wrapped with a robe." And Saul knew that it was Samuel, and he bowed with his face to the ground and did homage.

13. Then Samuel said to Saul, "Why have you disturbed me by bringing me up?" And Saul answered, "I am greatly distressed; for the Philistines are waging war against me, and God has departed from me and no longer answers me either through prophets or by dreams; therefore I have called you, that you may make known to me what I should do."

14. Samuel said, "Why then do you ask me, since the LORD has departed from you and has become your adversary?"

15. "The LORD has done accordingly as He spoke through me; for the LORD has torn the kingdom out of your hand and given it to your neighbor, to David."

16. "As you did not obey the LORD and did not execute His fierce wrath on Amalek, so the LORD has done this thing to you this day."

17. "Moreover the LORD will also give over Israel along with you into the hands of the Philistines; therefore tomorrow you and your sons will be with me. Indeed the LORD will give over the army of Israel into the hands of the Philistines!"

18. Then Saul immediately fell full length upon the ground and was very afraid because of the words of

Samuel; also there was no strength in him, for he had eaten no food all day and all night.

19. The woman came to Saul and saw that he was terrified, and said to him, "Behold, your maidservant has obeyed you, and I have taken my life in my hand and have listened to your words which you spoke to me."

20. "So now also, please listen to the voice of your maidservant, and let me set a piece of bread before you that you may eat and have strength when you go on your way."

21. But he refused and said, "I will not eat." However, his servants together with the woman urged him, and he listened to them. So he arose from the ground and sat on the bed.

22. The woman had a fattened calf in the house, and she quickly slaughtered it; and she took flour, kneaded it and baked unleavened bread from it.

23. She brought it before Saul and his servants, and they ate. Then they arose and went away that night.

Chapters 29 and 30 of First Samuel are about David and his conversations and arguments with Achish the Philistine king. The Philistines had taken David in, despite his killing of their warrior, Goliath. Achish had a kinship and liking toward David and protected him from King Saul when Saul was upset that the people of Israel had taken up with David instead of him. Besides wanting to eliminate the Philistines, Saul was also hell bent on eliminating David. Chapters 29 and 30 report the conversations between Achish and David where Achish says his fight is with Saul and the Israelites and that David is to stay in the rear of his armies. This leads to Chapter 31:

1. Now the Philistines were fighting against Israel, and the men of Israel fled from before the Philistines and fell slain on Mount Gilboa.

2. *The Philistines overtook Saul and his sons; and the Philistines killed Jonathan (*formerly David's best friend*) along with Abinadab and Malchi-Shua, the sons of Saul.*

3. *The battle went heavily against Saul, and the archers hit him; and he was badly wounded by the archers.*

4. *Then Saul said to his armor bearer, "Draw your sword and pierce me through with it, otherwise these uncircumcised will come and pierce me through and make sport of me." But his armor bearer would not, for he was greatly afraid. So Saul took his sword and fell on it.*

5. *When his armor bearer saw that Saul was dead, he also fell on his sword and died with him.*

6. *Thus Saul died with his three sons, his armor bearer, and all his men on that day together.*

7. *When the men of Israel who were on the other side of the valley, with those who were beyond the Jordan, saw that the men of Israel had fled and that Saul and his sons were dead, they abandoned the cities and fled; then the Philistines came and lived in them.*

This is a story that seems to be on the minds of the pastors that Marisa and I have tried to speak to. What I find distressing and discouraging is that our pastors and others who are strong in their faith seem to refer to this story, saying that Samuel was outraged at being taken from his slumber. But my argument is that this spiritess that Saul sought out actually turned out to be a prophetess because what Samuel said would happen did happen. There was no untruth in his dialogue with Saul. The spiritess, to me, was as much a prophet to Saul as Gad was to David. Gad is glorified through eternity and the name of the spiritess is withheld but also glorified through eternity by having her story immortalized in text.

111

Throughout the Bible and the Koran, men of God seek out the Lord for help and guidance. When the guidance comes, it comes in dreams and in real human apparitions. Somehow, the distinctions between medium, spiritist, and prophet get muddled. These men and women of God that figuratively put their fingers in front of mine and Marisa's face with their index fingers crossed as if they are shielding themselves from evil seem to be unaware that there is little difference between someone like Marisa and the prophets of old. God is trying to teach us something that we can pass along to others so they can understand what is going on around them and to learn Truth.

In the New Testament, specifically in the books of Acts and Luke, Peter is released from prison by "angels" in human form. After the crucifixion of Jesus, his apostles are in the town square worshipping Jesus when they are arrested and put into jail.

Acts 5:17-25:

17. But the high priest rose up, along with all his associates (that is the sect of the Sadducees), and they were filled with jealousy.

18. They laid hands on the apostles and put them in a public jail.

19. But during the night an angel of the Lord opened the gates of the prison and taking them out he said,

20. "Go, stand and speak to the people in the temple the whole message of this Life."

21. Upon hearing this, they entered into the temple about daybreak and began to teach. Now when the high priest and the associates came, they called the Council together, even all the Senate of the sons of Israel, and sent orders to the prison house for them to be brought.

22. But the officers who came did not find them in the prison; and they returned and reported back,

23. *Saying, "We found the prison house locked quite securely and the guards standing at the doors; but when we had opened up, we found no one inside."*

24. *Now when the captain of the temple guard and the chief priests heard these words, they were greatly perplexed about them as to what would come of this.*

25. *But someone came and reported to them, "The men whom you put in prison are standing in the temple and teaching the people!"*

An angel of the Lord took on human form and in some strange way was able to either open the doors of the jail and make the disciples either invisible or to somehow make time stand still while he opened the gates of the prison so the apostles could run out. Then he closed the prison and let time start again. The prison guards had continued to stand guard at the prison gates.

Since this was initially written, I have had a further clarification of what actually transpired. They said that the energy of the Spirits of the disciples entered the energies of the guards and "hypnotized" them to open the gates. Once the disciples were safely gone, the Spirits that assisted the disciples by merely "snapping their fingers," and the guards were back as they were, no wiser for what they had done. Therefore, when they were interrogated by their superiors, the guards just scratched their heads, so to speak. They didn't have a clue that they were responsible for freeing the disciples.

In Acts 7:51-60, Stephen, the first Christian martyr who was slain by Paul (who was Saul...but not the same Saul as in the previous story and later changed his name to Paul after being famously confronted by the risen Jesus on the road to Damascus) is speaking to the high priests of the Hellenistic Jews shortly after the Crucifixion. (The Jewish religion was already splintering between the Hellenistic Jews and the Native Jews.) Receiving guidance from the Lord, Stephen said:

> 51. *"You men who are stiff-necked and uncircumcised in heart and ears are always resisting the Holy Spirit; you are doing just as your fathers did.*
> 52. *"Which one of the prophets did your fathers not persecute? They killed those who had previously announced the coming of the "Righteous One", whose betrayers and murderers you have now become;*
> 53. *"You who received the law as ordained by angels, and yet did not keep it."*
> 54. *Now when they heard this, they were cut to the quick, and they began gnashing their teeth at him.*
> 55. *But being full of the Holy Spirit, he gazed intently into heaven and saw the glory of God, and Jesus standing at the right hand of God;*
> 56. *And he said, "Behold, I see the heavens opened up and the Son of Man standing at the right hand of God."*
> 57. *But they cried out with a loud voice, and covered their ears and rushed at him with one impulse.*
> 58. *When they had driven him out of the city, they began stoning him; and the witnesses laid aside their robes at the feet of a young man named Saul.*
> 59. *They went on stoning Stephen as he called on the LORD and said, "Lord Jesus, receive my spirit!"*
> 60. *Then falling on his knees, he cried out with a loud voice, "Lord, do not hold this sin against them!" Having said this, he fell asleep.*

What I have a problem with is that the spoken words of Stephen are taken as sacrosanct today. Stephen had visions of Jesus standing next to Christ in Heaven. He lamented that the Jews had persecuted the prophets that preceded him. So, as I stand next to a Christian who gives me the look and is holding

114

the two index fingers together as a cross so as not to be persecuted for listening to what Marisa and I have to say, I feel like I am Stephen speaking to the Hellenistic Jews who stoned him.

The Bible is filled with prophets and prophetesses who have dreams, visions, or visitations from angels who have taken human form and communicated with them. I feel that Marisa is no less a prophetess. I say this not in tones of blasphemy, but because I know that Marisa is in love with Christ, our God, and the Holy Spirit. Marisa is blessed with the ability to not only converse with angels and guides, but also able to meet with the deceased loved ones of grieving human souls. Marisa has brought more people to faith and trust in God than I will ever be able to do.

I tip my hat to the pastors that get up every day to help soothe their parishioners through blind faith. Those who come to the Lord God today do so out of faith that He is there. They trust that if they say prayers, God will listen and respond to their petitions. In the past, I just wasn't sure I was praying to anything but my own self, to my own mind and ego. Even though I have been baptized and felt the Holy Spirit awakened in me, I still didn't understand. I tried and tried, but my prayers always seemed to go unanswered and sometimes I felt that I was no better than the atheists who believe we're all just headed for a box in the ground. But that couldn't be farther from reality.

Eden interrupted only after I finished this chapter, which meant to me that they concur with everything I wrote. But Eden went on to say, "You don't need to put this in the book if you don't choose to but the Holy Spirit, the "Light", lives within every human being. But those who have not discovered the light within go about living "their free will" in such a way that would be considered "human evil" such as those actions that would be considered against the laws established by men. When one breaks one of the human laws, one can begin to dim the light within. When one's light is dimmed completely then that is when they will have to suffer the consequences on this side."

They kept saying that darkness cannot exist within the light. Nonetheless, when this was being spoken to me, my eyes welled up. I knew the Holy Spirit was happy that I understood what they were saying. As Jesus said in the little-known Book of Thomas (I'm paraphrasing), When confronted by human evil you must still respect and love the light that lives within that adversary, but, have the wisdom to turn away from it when it is clear that the light has been extinguished. This ties together the so-called instinct of men to "fight or fly," which is the way of a human mind, body and ego. It boils down to love and wisdom, light and dark, yin and yang, sowing and reaping.

Testimonials

I want to get further into what Heaven and Hell are, at least how they have been described to me through Marisa. But first, there are many people who have lost loved ones and have heard from them through Marisa. Like Saul seeking Samuel, they come to find out how their loved ones are doing in Heaven. So much goes unsaid when someone passes away suddenly. Wives, husbands, sons, all feel like there is unfinished business. I didn't know, for example, why my dad didn't tell me about his Bronze Star. We humans want to know that our passed loved ones are safe in Heaven. We want to know that we will have a place to go when we also pass on, and not just go "somewhere" but what life was all about in the first place. What we find out is nothing short of mind boggling when we go home.

In the movie *Gladiator*, the leading character, Maximus, always knew that he could live a life of fighting after his wife and son were murdered by his enemy and former brother-in-law, the Roman emperor. He lived that way knowing that one day he would go home. This was during the lifetime of Christ, when there were many gods. Knowing that there is something greater than this life gives us hope in this life that God will always be with us.

God has our back.

Following are testimonials sent to us by people who have come to Marisa.

Randy and Lisa Moris

My wife and I live in Mobile, Alabama, and have tried to live faithful Christian lives for many years. Although it is very difficult for many Christians to grasp the idea of what is on the "other side," and since I have taught for many years, I have been totally aware of the unseen world. By faith I believe that God, His Son Jesus, the Holy Spirit, and the multitude of angels have my back and care what happens to us each day. Marisa, through her work, has opened up this unseen world in a way that seemed unbelievable on one hand but totally believable on the other. My wife's father died on New Year's Eve of 2011, and in the few months prior, Marisa had helped us to know that a couple of siblings were indeed in Heaven. It excited us to know that Lisa's dad, who is a godly man, would be in Heaven but would actually be more alive than ever, and through Marisa, we have been able to get through a very difficult transition of losing a wonderful man. The work that Marisa has been called into and trained to do is truly a gift.

Kim Buske

Marisa is such a gift to all those whose paths bring them to her. I see her consistently touching those who work with her in ways that profoundly change their lives. Personally speaking, my life has been transformed in the year that I have been working with Marisa. She is such a clear channel in allowing my amazing guides to communicate their loving guidance, and she has taught me that I, too, can see and communicate with this high vibrational spiritual support team. I came from a place of not knowing anything about this other dimensional reality, and now not only am I a believer, but it has changed my life, my perspective, my sense of Self, and my strength of purpose. Marisa is a highly gifted intuitive and healer. She delivers spiritual messages from a place of sincere humility, purity of heart, and perceptive wisdom that cuts through illusive walls.

Megan Valentine

I met Marisa through my dad. My dad and her dad play golf together. I was struggling with my gift of seeing spirits at night when I was trying to sleep. I had gone with very little sleep for about two weeks and had a frightening experience one night and shared all that had been happening to me with my dad. He suggested I contact Marisa, based on what her dad (Joe) had shared about her. I also had been feeling anxiety with my dog, which had come from an abusive past and was acting out all of a sudden. So I and my dog went to Marisa's office, not knowing what to expect. She was so warm and loving and made me feel so comforted right away. She worked on my dog first and told me all about her abusive past and that she was clearing the emotional cords from her previous owner and from my soon to be ex-husband which were causing her sadness and pain.

Keep in mind I was a skeptic and didn't quite know what to think of all this. Then she moved on to me and told me things she could not have known no matter how much she may have Googled me (haha). She cleared out my emotional cords, taught me how to clear my house of spirits and how I was in control of what spirits can and cannot do in my life. I went away feeling so much lighter and peaceful. It was truly amazing. I went home, did the cleansing ritual, and was able to sleep peacefully every night since then. I also felt an amazing sense of peace and love for myself and even for my ex-husband. After I felt all that, I became a firm believer in all she did. After a few days my family saw a huge change in me that two of my sisters, my niece and nephew, my brother-in-law and a friend of mine all were

119

inspired to go see Marisa. Each of them has now been healed through Marisa as well.

I also went back a second time so I could learn to clear all my negative energy that I take on from others throughout my day. I have been able, through Marisa's teachings, to do this on my own, which has completely changed my life. I was on meds for sleeping and for anxiety, but after seeing Marisa, I am no longer on any medications. I am able to rid all negative energy that comes my way and live the best life that I have always desired to live. God has given Marisa an amazing gift, and I am thankful she is using it to heal people and bring them closer to Him. I love being able to call on my angels and guides for help and protection. I never knew they had always been there just for me. I just needed to believe and ask.

Marisa has completely changed my mindset and given me the tools to make my life the very best it can be. Through all this, she has brought my family much closer to each other and our conversations have changed from all the hardships we have in life, to all the blessings we have now and all we are learning. Thank you Marisa, we love you and we are so thankful God placed you in our lives at just the right time...

Molly Chase

I've gained more from working with Marisa in four months than I have in years of traditional therapies. Thanks to her gifts, I have gained a deeper sense of self awareness that has unlocked new life inside of me. Her lessons have enabled me to feel more confident, focused, energetic, and powerful than I've felt in my whole life. Plus, my anxiety is now practically non-existent, and I'm sleeping like a baby after years of restless sleeping!

Michelle Powers

Marisa Moris has a true gift of intuition, perception, healing and love! After two of my sisters were helped by her, I decided to see her for myself. She is wise and discerning beyond her years...she helped me (and later my husband) uncover the root of what we have been feeling. Like a lot of people, we have experienced grief, loss, surgery, a move, family issues, career changes, etc., just in the past year alone! This left us rattled and uncertain...however with Marisa's gift of channeling spirit messages; she seeks to help with our highest good in mind.

I appreciate Marisa's audio recording of our sessions...I was able to go back and listen more intently and learn from the info she channeled for me. I highly recommend Marisa to anyone with a spiritually open and curious mind...you will be amazed, encouraged, and healed. Thanks, Marisa...keep up the good work! ♥

Marla Anthony

I had a Reiki session with Marisa Moris on June 9, 2012, that changed my life. Twenty-eleven was one of the hardest years of my life. My grandmother, who I was very close to, died in June. In August, we were at our worst financially, my husband got a new job that took him away for sometimes ten hours a day while my four-year-old son stopped going to preschool and was home with me full time. In the same month, my twelve-year-old son started junior high. In October, my father-in-law, who I was very close to, died.

Needless to say, the first death in June hit me very hard. I was with my grandmother when she took her last breath, and that was the first time I ever experienced death. I didn't realize how much I was affected by that until I got home. I started feeling depressed and missed my grandma very much. Then in August, when my husband got a new job, son home full-time,

121

other son starting junior high and father-in-law passing away two months later was when I hit bottom and my hope for happiness was gone again. I couldn't see anything positive. I was raised with God as being the hope and praying to him would change my life. I tried that, along with the help of my family, but I think I was so far gone I couldn't see any light at all.

The advice I was getting from people who loved me was taken as a burden instead of hope. I was stuck in my pit and didn't know how I was going to survive. I eventually got to a point where I wanted to go beyond and not come back. Heaven looked like my way out of my depression. The only thing that held me here was my two boys. Then one of my sisters went to see Marisa, and I saw her life changing experience, and then it hit me. This is exactly what I needed.

I made an appointment with Marisa and met with her and it changed my life. She told me that I am a magnet with people's energy. I learned a lot from them and what they had to tell me. I learned about all my guides and angels that are always with me. I left that Reiki reading/medium session with a renewed spirit. I felt like I had been reborn and had a positive outlook on life and realized my gift that I am now pursing.

God used Marisa to change my life. I will forever be grateful to her and God and all those who loved me by showing up and helping me find that hope again.

Marisa said I was covered in it so much that it took her a while to find my energy. Almost immediately, though, I felt better. Marisa then brought up some things from my past that I needed to be healed from. She told me about my family and the cords I had with them. She gave me the tools to continue with my healing and how to protect my own energy. I even had my grandmother and father-in-law come into the reading and I got complete closure with their deaths.

Jenny Kurth

*For many years, since I was a young child, God and my existence have fascinated me completely **and** overwhelmingly so. I was raised in a Christian family, yet was always questioning my elders about why there are so many religions. Wasn't there just one God? I was taught that all other religions were evil when I inquired about them, and felt saddened no one could answer me about what was going on and why I was living on earth, a planet in space. Even at a young age, this confused me, as I thought we're all the same, so how could we condemn each other's beliefs? What do you believe when everyone claims their religion is the only one? I kinda gave up. Well, yeah, I gave up.*

I spent many years inwardly searching and couldn't find anything that truly made sense to me, except that God exists. I felt I had no direction in my life. I viewed myself as just a painfully shy passerby with no point in a society driven by degrees and careers; I only wanted to be a mom. I became severely depressed for years and was diagnosed with bi-polar disorder, manic-depressive disorder, even schizophrenia. I was prescribed countless medications and rarely had a doctor counsel me. I felt they didn't know anything about me, didn't care to know, and were just feeding me pills for a quick fix and a high price.

I started a life of self-medicating with alcohol and illegal drugs, which resulted in hospitalizations and abusive relationships with men and with my own spirit. This period of my life lasted thirteen years until unemployment had me at home day and night studying for my reason to exist--again, extensively. And then, I met Marisa.

A friend of mine told me she had seen Marisa for an intuitive Reiki healing and how eye-opening it was for her. Not being familiar with what an intuitive Reiki healing was my friend went on to describe how Marisa had the ability to connect with not only the true spirit inside of us, but our Higher Self, our spirit guides and teachers, angels, and archangels. If this wasn't

123

mind blowing enough, she could also see and remove energetic cords to people, places, and things which no longer served a person's life. I immediately felt a lightning bolt come through my body, head to toe. At that point, I had chills all over my body, running through my spine, and I knew in my heart I must meet her. This was my sign.

After meeting with Marisa for the first time, I FINALLY felt that someone truly understood me and could help me. I learned that I am an empathic medium and that I have a high sensitivity to energies. This explained so much for me, to know why growing up and still to this day I would be so overcome by others around me. I would take on others' energy and confuse it with my own emotions and mental state. She taught me how to protect myself and relayed messages from my Higher Self that it is so important to become aware of my own energy so that I may know what is mine and what is not. She helped me find a light switch that I knew was there somewhere...hiding in a dark room which I had forgotten about. She helped me to remember the goals and purpose of my life. When she spoke to me from my Higher Self, it was like she was describing everything about me that no one knew. Some things that were even hard for me to admit. She helped me to realize the self-abuse I had inflicted upon myself was ego-driven and that once I heal myself, I will be living my purpose of being a healer and a teacher. Marisa has taught me that when I merge with my true spirit, trust in my Divine plan, and have patience with my mind and body and know I am part of God, what do I really need to worry about? I am learning. She serves in the light of Christ as my Reiki master, healer, counselor, teacher, and a dear friend. I feel blessed to walk with her as we open our eyes to reality as it really exists. I have never felt so alive in my thirty-five years, where things just seem to synchronize and make sense. Every day is literally a new day and I can't seem to say to her enough.

THANK YOU, MARISA! You are truly a gift from God in my life.

Shelly

I am a forty-six-year-old hair stylist in Temecula, California. I truly love my job of making people feel beautiful, hopefully inside and out. After twenty-two years of marriage, two amazing kids that are now married and doing great, I am single and searching for my new journey in life! Recently, I was at a place where I was lost, hopeless, depressed, and alone. My bright light was now very dim.

I was told about Marisa by a client of mine who met with Marisa last year with amazing results. I said I NEED HER NOW, PLEASE!!! When I called Marisa, we connected right away and couldn't stop talking... So I made an appointment, even though I didn't have the money. I actually took it from my car payment. Shhh! Obviously, my priority at the time was my life/health over my car payment. I came in that Sunday as a broken, hopeless, desperate soul trying to find my path.

I've never had a Reiki healing done on myself, but was very interested. I had hope, being a Christian and very curious in what is really on the other side. I met my angel guide about three years ago and have been kind of searching ever since. The minute Marisa laid her hands on my head, being in her presence made me feel so secure and at peace. As she continued the Reiki healing she soon realized how damaged I was. My light was out!! Not good and not me!

Being a hair stylist is very rewarding, but also very draining, sometimes, being more mental than physical. Laying my hands on clients' heads (crown chakras) every day can be very draining. I take in their negative/positive energy. But I don't know how to reboot or protect myself from those energies. As Marisa went down my damaged and clogged chakras, she was reading me and at the same time helping understand and clear all my chakras!!! OMG Amazing!!! As Marisa met my guide, passed family that came through, and all of our friendly visitors,

125

I was feeling lighter and lighter by each hour! Yes, four hours later, I was a FULL NEW SOUL with a purpose and bright new path!

Marisa's mix of her Reiki healing gift and her connection with her guides as well as mine cleansed my soul and heart like I've never felt before. It was almost 9:00 p.m., and I wanted to run down the street screaming, "I am new again!!!" I felt fifty pounds lighter and ready to take on the world. But I didn't want to freak Marisa out! Lol.

Marisa is truly a GIFT from God! I will always have a huge place in my heart for her. I am so very excited to start and share my new journey with her. I cannot wait to take her Reiki classes to soak up everything I will have to offer in the healing world. Since I have been doing it by touching clients' heads and giving advice all day, I thought I should learn from the best to expand my love for healing and learn how to protect myself and much, much more.

I just want to say a huge THANK YOU Marisa and cannot wait to see what the future holds. Please continue healing and blessing others with your amazing gift and love for wounded souls.

Stacy Aguilera

I met Marisa in December of 2012 and it wasn't by chance. I was really struggling with my life because I didn't understand my purpose for being on this earth. All I experienced anymore seemed to be emotional pain. My husband used to say to me that I didn't like him and at the time he was right because I didn't like myself. I was seeking self-help in so many ways, but nothing was helping. I remember crying out to God begging for answers, begging for my pain to go away. I wanted anything to stop the pain even if it meant not living anymore and two days later, I met Marisa. Marisa changed my life. She was able to answer so many questions I had about life. The funny part was they were answers I knew all along, but she confirmed my beliefs and helped give me some guidance and purpose. Immediately after this, I got a Reiki healing and since then I'm much better. I still have a way to go, but I'm finally happy again. I'm in love with my husband again. I can see now that I never allowed him to love me and now I can because I'm starting to love myself more and more each day.

I've stopped going to self-help meetings, off anti-depressants, and no longer need a psychiatrist. Instead I am pursuing Reiki and learning how to connect spiritually and self-heal. I am starting to progress toward my purpose and I'm happy. To some of you, I may seem like an extreme case and others may relate, but what I do know is I wouldn't be where I am today if I never met Marisa. She is a Light in this dark world and I say that sincerely from the bottom of my heart. Thank you, Marisa. I am forever grateful that God and all my angels and guides brought you into my life.

Ana Girdner

I met Joe Moris two years ago when he walked into my real estate office in Punta de Mita, Mexico. He asked if he could use my office to make a phone call. That was the beginning of our business partnership as well as our friendship. We started talking about the real estate market in Mexico, which led me to tell him that I had shared our office until just recently, with my late husband, Don Girdner, who to everyone's shock was diagnosed with an inoperable brain tumor on November 1, 2010. It was shocking as he was so full of personality, energy, and life. So much so that he earned the nickname Superman in our little town, as he so much resembled Clark Kent. After days in the intensive care unit of a premier hospital in Puerto Vallarta, I decided to take him home and continue his care there. He passed away on December 28 after much pain and suffering. I was devastated, as he was the center of my life, both as a spouse and

127

business partner. The entire community came together when he got sick and raised money for his medical care as we did not have medical insurance. It was then that I realized that this was my true home where all my friends and neighbors are.

Joe mentioned his daughter, Marisa, to me and the special gift that she had in communicating with those who had departed our world. There was a real sadness that was apparent to everyone. I made a trip to San Diego in June of 2011, and Joe encouraged me to meet with Marisa. He even treated me to a Reiki healing with her. Marisa felt Don's presence around me from the moment she met me. She let me know that he had been looking for someone on this earth to communicate with me ever since he left. I have a sister who is an energy healer in Venice Beach. He had tried to communicate with her, but she kept on rejecting his presence (they never got along, those two). So it was Don who brought Joe to my life and through him, Marisa.

During my session with Marisa, he appeared. She described him as well as his mannerisms to the T. He let me know that he was happy, had connected with his mentor in Heaven (Joe), was playing lots of golf (one of his passions), and had met my dad, who had passed away twelve years prior. He enjoyed long conversations with him. He reassured me not to worry any more, that he was very happy and that we would connect soon again. During that same session, six other spirits appeared; my dad, my grandmother on my mothers' side, my grandmother on my father's side (whom I had never met. She passed away when my dad was eleven), and my uncle Richard. Marisa described them all. She said that my dad had always wanted to tell me how very proud he was of me, but that he never did and wanted me to finally know. It was a surreal experience, especially my communication with the spirits who are always with me. I have encountered death with only three people who were so very dear to me and who influenced who I am today: my Dad, Don, and my grandmother on my mother's side.

That session with Marisa changed me, as it gave me closure with Don in knowing that he is happy and in a better

*place. After my return to Punta de Mita, Mexico, my friends
noticed a remarkable change in me. They all told me how bright
I now looked as opposed to the sadness that I had been carrying
for so many months. I thank Marisa for that, and I look forward
to many more sessions with her. God bless you.*

These are just a few of the testimonials that we have
received from the many who have met with Marisa. There is
calmness and a sense of God and His light that surrounds Marisa.
She is not afraid or embarrassed to praise God and His huge
administration for being in our lives. Knowing the linkage we
have to the Father is comforting, but there is a dark side, too.
This can be very scary because there is truly a spiritual war
taking place that is so powerful and beyond our immediate
understanding.

The Bible tells us of this spiritual battle, but like anything
else, experiencing the darkness can be very unnerving. Marisa
has been told that unlike the prophets of old, she is not allowed
to tell the future. Marisa's Lord or Higher Self has lived many
lives, including one that is so recognizable that I'm not going to
name her, but most of her previous lives were planned to be a
teacher as she is here. Unfortunately, in the murky past, anyone
with Marisa's abilities would immediately be labeled a heretic or
a witch. In the Old Testament, she would have been labeled as a
spiritist and been stoned to death.

Marisa is very careful about asking Christ and her lineage
to be with her whenever she allows her energy to be lifted in
order to communicate with the other side. On the other side,
there are spirits that are not always for our highest and best.
Sometimes these other spirits can be downright scary.

A friend of Marisa's said that he had a friend in
Hollywood with a very large mansion. The man in Hollywood
was well connected with the film industry. Shortly after
purchasing the home he lives in, he felt that there was a presence
in the home, and it didn't feel good at all. He is not a spiritual
person, but he knew that he wasn't safe in his own home. One

day, this man was about to come down the stairs in his home. The staircase was expansive and winding, as one would expect in a $15 million mansion in the heart of Beverly Hills. At that moment, he hesitated. He was ready to return to his bedroom for something he had forgotten when he felt a heavy hand in the middle of his back give him a violent shove. He fell down the entire staircase. Since he lived alone, there was no one there to come to his aid. He was knocked unconscious and lay at the bottom of the stairs for some time before he had the ability to find his way to a phone and call 911 for help.

When another acquaintance of Marisa's told him about Marisa, he was in the hospital with a broken pelvis, one broken leg, and multiple cracked ribs, along with cuts and abrasions. He was also scared to death. He did not want to go back to his home. He asked if Marisa would go to the house to see if it was possessed. When Marisa was contacted about going through the home, she initially refused. Finally, she was talked into it by her friend.

When Marisa entered the home, she knew she was in the presence of darkness, even though no one in particular came through immediately. Marisa instantly asked for Christ's Shield and His Light and began saying the Lord's Prayer. An apparition of a large man appeared at the top of the stairs. The man looked at Marisa and laughed. He asked Marisa if she thought the Lord's Prayer would save her. Marisa said, "Yes." The man just laughed and told her that he wasn't afraid of God; that this was his house, and he wasn't leaving. Then he told Marisa to get out.

When what Marisa calls "hitch-hikers" come in unexpectedly during a Reiki healing with someone, all she has to do is say, "Hey, get out of here!" Because Marisa has the strength of the universe with her, the "hitch-hikers" usually just drop their chins and skulk away. Most are harmless and are thrilled to see Marisa's portal to the other side. As most of them say, it is like hitting the celestial lottery to come back and communicate with living humans, and even though they are not invited, they just want to be in on the action. These are typically souls that have not yet crossed over through the Light but are not evil, either. Many are Souls that took their own lives and are afraid to go through the Light and be punished by God.

At the time of this writing, that is exactly where the football player is. According to our conversations, this football star is very mad at himself for taking his own life and continues to this day to attempt in some way to bring peace to all those who loved him before he committed suicide. He won't go through the Light until someone tells him it is now okay to go. In the meantime, family members may sense his presence at times because he really is there trying to communicate, but he can't. Not unless he finds someone like Marisa who will encourage him to go find his real home through the Light.

Back to the example: This evil man who stood at the top of the stairs had enough evil energy to actually become partly visible in human form and have the ability to push the occupant of his home down the stairs. This made every hair on Marisa's body stand straight up. She and her friend immediately vacated the house. Nothing she said to convince this man to go through the Light was fruitful. This man loved his Hell and wasn't about to leave. Marisa left the mansion, told the owner of the house there was nothing she could do, and convinced him to sell the home and move. She said tearing the mansion down did no good, as the apparition would just take residence in any new home built there.

Evil is truly scary. It is all around us. This world belonged to Lucifer. He was initially a bright morning star in God's legions. Unfortunately, at the coming of Adam and Eve, Lucifer chose to be like God. He chose to be in competition for God's created souls. Lucifer has his own worlds in this universe and, unfortunately, Earth is one of them. According to *The Urantia Book*, Lucifer has thirty-six planets that are inhabited by humans of his own creation, but the actual physical presence of Hell remains in the lower astral or lower etheric realm.[7] As I

---

[7] I still haven't quite figured out the difference. I think the "etheric body" is

mentioned earlier, the etheric realm is the place we all go while in transition to home, or Heaven, as we call it. But the etheric realm is also where Hell is. There are seven layers of Hell, and the top layer is filled with former humans that have had enough of Lucifer and Satan and want to work their way back to Heaven. This is where God allows evil to coexist with good. The earth has a soul and lives on the second level. New souls, evolving from other mammals and becoming human start out on the earth's second level of God's ever-eternal quest to the seventh level. This is the level where graduating souls from Hell get to work for their salvation here on Earth, but don't forget—all souls, good and bad, come to earth with amnesia. Therefore, God allows good and bad to coexist on earth. Although Earth is in the outermost part of this universe, far away from level four and up, planets like those in Pleiades and Arcturus, Earth may actually be considered the center of the universe. For in this galaxy, Earth is the only planet that God has allowed levels two through six spirits to coexist in duality.

This was my initial obsession when I chose to support Marisa in her God-given abilities. I had to know that there were consequences for evil and hopes that our natural human tendencies were not so severe that we all ended up in Hell. Besides, I couldn't understand how someone, another spirit, could attain such a high level, such as a level five or level six like Benjamin Franklin or Albert Einstein, and then in their human condition of a Lucifer influence on earth, cause them to recede back into level one and, worse yet, end up in level seven

my whole body, including all the layers of auras I have. The "astral body" is the part of the body that can leave at night while you are asleep and deliver itself back into the astral realm to converse with our friends who are watching and taking care of each of us. That is when our spirit departs us and plans our next day or week. That is why sometimes you have déjà vu moments. You have them when you physically do something exactly the way it was planned. You will have a déjà vu moment because you had already programmed the possibility of that incident happening into your subconscious by your spirit, the real you that eventually goes home when the earthly vessel gives out and the amnesia goes away.

of Hell, where Hitler and Pol Pot are, along with many other despicable human beings.

Hell

Wanting to make sure that Marisa and I are not working in the darkness, I had to know that there is a Hell for humans that are truly evil. There just had to be a place that was a punishment for humans who did not find the Love and Light of Christ while human and that there are consequences for the evil they inflict on others. But evil has to be identified before a judgment can be made. While we live in our various religious or irreligious boxes, we create rules to be followed or broken, and sometimes we create our own Hell right here on earth by condemning ourselves for what are, basically, manmade rules.

I remember meeting my wife, Gleda, in 1972 while I was in the army. She was attending a Baptist college. Our first date was to a pizza parlor with a bunch of my buddies and their girlfriends. When we went back to her dorm, I suggested we play a game of cards, but she said that her faith didn't permit card playing, that it was evil and she would go to Hell. Gleda and those of her faith at that time and place in Texas were creating their own hell. If someone in her college played cards, then the guilt they felt would be enough to drive them away from the church and God.

Many people, when they realize they are in this little spiritual or ideological box, choose to climb out of the box and live the life that is occurring all around them, the secular life. They join most of society by living a secular life, which in reality is where Lucifer's playground is. It is in the secular life that you find what most of us would characterize as evil, such as the pursuit of worldly treasures instead of Heavenly treasures. That is, they're seeking things over compassion for others.

I asked Gleda to at least go to a dance with me, but she said if she danced, she would go to Hell. Eventually, she broke out of the box she was in and we got married and moved to Santa Barbara, where I went to college. She saw that I had no box around me and joined me in the world...the world that is influenced by Lucifer.[8]

Gleda and I lived a good life far away from God for many years until my curiosity got the best of me and in 1998, I was baptized in the light. We were married in 1974, so we both lived primarily away from God for twenty-four years. We weren't bad people; we just didn't know God. After my baptism, my wife followed me in spirit and also lived her life to glorify God.

Living away from God and the light leads us to be influenced by Lucifer, even though we are not aware of it. As explained in *The Urantia Book*, Lucifer and Satan are still being judged by a heavenly Supreme Court, which they call the Ancient of Days (Matthew 5:21, Daniel 7:9). Members of this heavenly Supreme Court are humans who have graduated all the way to the seventh level and sit at the right hand of Christ as Christed Souls. Lucifer goes to work to make our life a living hell, while God and his legion of former humans and His created angels try to fill us with the blessings of Heaven on earth. We will find the good, and when we see the evil, we will have a chance to spread our light to these unknowing spirits in hopes of bringing over these lost souls to the goodness that is innate in their lives.

---

[8] This turned out to be the most spirited part of an entire year of conversations with the other side. The end of the sentence reads "influenced by Lucifer." I had originally written "controlled by Lucifer" and cited examples, like the story (Matthew 4:1-11) of Christ being in the wilderness for forty days and forty nights and being tempted by Satan, where Satan opened his arms and offered all the kingdoms of the world to Jesus, and all Jesus had to do was to kneel and worship at the feet of Satan. That's when Christ responded, "Be gone Satan! For it is written, 'you shall not put the Lord your God to the test'." My response was; *how can anyone give anything away that isn't owned?* My claim was that Lucifer/Satan/the Devil controls the earth. This was a real no-no with the "other side." I actually ended up in an argument with the guys on the other side. Of course, they are right. The earth belongs to God and is controlled by Christ, and Lucifer happens to be just a part of it.

They said that this book is about education, education in the Light. They felt that portraying this world as something owned by Lucifer was flat out wrong and, finally, to put it in a way that my simple mind could understand, they called Lucifer a sort of manager who went power mad (my own term, just to sum it up).

135

As I stated at the beginning of this book, Earth is a sort of Petrie dish where we individually are our Lord/Higher Selves. On a personal level, my Lord created a fraction of Himself in Spirit, and that became me. My Higher Self/Lord becomes me. I have come to learn that my Soul multiplies itself and thus has experienced many lives through its created spirits, one of which is me right now as I write this. In all the good that is experienced through the human experience, I am able to graduate to higher levels in Heaven as long as I don't screw up and put myself in Hell. According to our teachers and guides, we humans think linearly, and linear thinking is all we really understand. They have explained that there are seven levels of development with a boatload of levels within each level, all having to deal with attempting to complete a life exactly as we planned it in spirit and in conjunction with all our loved ones up there prior to becoming human.

Level one is Hell, Earth is level two. Level seven is where Christ resides with all the graduated spirits and souls. I can say that the likes of Moses, Daniel, Paul, John, Isaiah, Elisha, and Elijah have all graduated to the governing councils in Christ's administration. I've learned that my own Lord/Higher Self has graduated to the fourth level. That is what the real me is, a fourth-level spirit/soul growing ever closer to rejoining my real Soul, who was created by my Oversoul, who was created by Christ. I am told that there is no way to describe levels above what we have earned unless they are described to the Higher Self while in Heaven by those who have attained that level, and similar to the way our guides and my Lord and Higher Self are presenting the etheric realm to Marisa and me at this time as humans.

It is hard to grasp the magnificence of each level of Heaven, but we are reminded over and over again that there are many levels within each level. My dad has just graduated to the first level of the fourth level, my mom is a mid-third-level being, and Marisa and I both are high-fourth-level spirits. When one of our human existences causes us to go to Hell, then that results in

136

our Lord and Higher Self being unable to advance until such a time that that particular spirit is successful in graduating and transitioning out of Hell. Since my mom is still a part of my Soul Family and if everyone else in my nuclear soul group is a level four and above, and she is still a level three, then I can only assume that at some point she wasn't a very good girl in one of her lives. A piece of my soul could be stuck in Hell from a previous life as well, maybe even two. I won't know until I go home.

Think of two balloons filled with helium in a 10-foot by 10-foot room and both are released to fly up to the ceiling (simplistically this room equates to our astral/etheric realm, which means earth and all its dimensions). If one of those balloons has a very slight leak, then it will lag behind the other balloon, which will fly higher and faster. When our Soul experiences one life where the spirit is unable to locate the light and in essence creates so much anguish that it is considered being in Hell, then that is a drain on the energy of the soul. It causes the soul to be slower in its development. When the hell-bound spirit is absolved of its sins by working its way back to the light, think of it as patching the leak in the balloon and replacing the lost helium. The guides really liked the Helium Example:

Here is how they expanded on my helium example: What we would like to explain to you...is that the different levels of what you call Heaven, or as we call it, the "Soul Plane," are different levels all existing as one (think of the 10x10 room). Just as you may live on earth and experience Heaven or Hell, this is all consciousness-based. Life is experienced differently on the Soul Plane for each and every single person. So, just as you mentioned your mother in this incarnation, she still experiences life in the exact same place as your father is. Her light is just a little bit dimmer. So what we need to explain is that each soul needs to have a certain amount of voltage to experience life on...[she hesitated and then continued]...imagine this: just as you have used the wonderful balloon example, imagine a balloon with less helium in it that cannot rise as high. A balloon with more helium in it can rise much higher. These can all exist in the same room. Some may just be a little higher and some may be just a little lower. The balloons that are existing just a little bit higher may come together with the balloons that are existing a little lower, and in this case, say, 'Let's incarnate together and maybe learn a little something from me so that your balloon will have a little more helium so that we can lift up together.' This doesn't mean that the balloons that are ten feet up are in a separate room from balloons that may only be two or five or six feet up. They are all existing in the same room, and this is what the Soul Plane is. And in the soul "pods," the soul "families," and even the soul "groups," there are many helium balloons at different heights, some that are much higher and some that are much lower.

When a balloon reaches a certain height (the room's ceiling) with the helium, which in this case we call the Light of Christ [hesitation again], as each soul attains more light, or in this case, the balloon gathers more helium through life experiences, through turning their human life over to God, and experiencing pain and despair in a lifetime, but turning it over to God and learning how to manifest the life of their dreams, although they have an ego and emotions, they elect to block the helium from filling the balloon. As these balloons fill up with more helium, they go higher and higher and higher, but this doesn't mean they go to different places. They're all still in the same room, just as you were all on the same earth plane. But we still call it the "Soul Plane". It is just a physical plane of the soul plane. There are still souls on this plane, they just have, as we used in the last example, a statue, a physical manifestation of that soul. So please understand that each soul plane is not a different soul plane. They're all the same and all the different balloons exist in the same Soul Plane (same room).

Now when a certain balloon reaches certain fullness and reaches a certain height, it may decide to go live in a different room. And these other rooms would be the soul planes of other universes and other planets. They may choose to go live over there. There are an etheric and an astral realm. There is a soul plane for each planet. There are beings that live in the etheric realms of each planet that has physical beings on it. But this is something we will go into later. It will be covered in our next book. But please understand and know that just as an elementary school has grades K through 6, there are not different schools for different grades, and in this case, the soul plane, every soul and every level lives in the same place.

Our Soul doesn't die when one of the lives/spirits of the soul goes to Hell (which is really a portion of the lower astral/etheric realm). Our Soul just learns lessons it didn't intend or want to learn. This would be a lesson about going to Hell that the spirit learns about thanks to its right to act out on its own free will.

Since we have all lived before, in spirit, we have experienced many lives. Personally, I have been told that I lived a life during the days of Rome. I also lived during the Dark Ages, during the American Revolution, and I also worked as a blacksmith in the 1800s. I have also lived on a planet in the constellation of the Pleiades. That is a planet that only allows levels four through six to exist. It is a place where there is absolute beauty and peace. No level ones are there. Level one is Hell, but since the inhabitants of Hell are created souls by Lucifer, coupled with lost human souls created by the light who were unsuccessful in their ability to find the Holy Spirit in them while they were human, and thus created their own hells on earth with indescribable evil and horror, they, too, live in Hell with souls that were created by Lucifer to be evil.

Lucifer's created souls are not allowed to come to earth, but the souls created directly from Christ can graduate[9] back to earth after going to Hell. Yes, Hitler may actually work his way back to earth in a new human body someday, but he has a long

---

[9] They like to use the word "transition."

way to go. These souls can realize that their place in Hell is not what was designed for them, and they have the ability to work their way back through the various levels of Hell to get another chance to come to earth and attempt to accomplish preset goals and then earn their way back to Heaven from where they started. Unfortunately, with their inbred evil ways, most of the graduates of Hell find it hard or impossible with amnesia to break the cycle they themselves created when living away from the light.

God, therefore, allows evil to coexist with good. Again, Earth is like a Petrie dish in that God allows levels one through level six to coexist here on earth. That is why you see such horror and evil within the world and the righteous asking why God could allow such a thing to happen to good people. No one is forced to come back to earth to learn lessons, but those spirits, just like you and me, decided on their own, without any pressure from the other side that this is a good place to take a big chance to grow spiritually.

Snow Globe

In our first draft of this book, I spent hours upon hours transcribing the conversations, only to toss the whole thing. The recordings are readily available to be heard, but I begrudgingly agreed to put this book into my own words. I listened again to tens of hours of conversations with the other side. Leading into the conclusion, I just have to give to you, word for word, the snow globe example. I love it when they use examples like they are telling us parables. Here is the transcription of their Snow Globe example:

Eden and Jeremy: The light within each human being is strong, and the light in each human being is there. When you say "extinguishing that light," it can only be extinguished by, just as you've said, human emotions and those that man has deemed as wrong. What we would like to explain, though, is that some human beings feel that some things are wrong that are not really wrong with other human beings. So it really all depends upon the consciousness and rules that that human being was brought up in. Just as you've mentioned manmade laws, this makes a huge difference where a person is born and what kind of a society that this human is brought up in.

The Holy Spirit resides in each and every person, or as we call it, the Light. The Light is within; the Light is pure; the Light is strong; the Light is quite astounding, if I must say so myself. The Light is within us over here as well. This is the Guiding Light. This is the Morning Star that guides us through the physicality. This is the star that leads us through the ethers and through the heavenly realms.

When the soul is damaged, hurt, when the aura has holes in it, when the body is damaged, not just the physical body, but the emotional, mental, spiritual body, and those of the subtle bodies are damaged, the Light does not get dimmer. It just makes

141

it harder for the consciousness to see the Light; to see darkness, to see emotions, to see those things in the human field....

Marisa: Hold on, here's Yeshua.

Joe: Oh, wow, I wonder if he'll give me the parable He started the other day." The one I ended up interrupting, like an idiot, and He and we never got back to.

Yeshua: What we would like to explain to you is the Light coming from each and every Higher Self down into the physical body of that being is strong. Inside that physical being there is the Holy Spirit, the Soul. Inside that physical body, that Soul has experiences that have been carried throughout from past lives. The Holy Spirit is still strong within. By turning over the will, the life, to God, as you say, one is opening oneself up and allowing God to shine down into and through the crown chakra of the physical body, down through the energy centers, and connect with the Holy Spirit within. See this field as a big globe, a big snow globe. The light shining from above is God, is Christ, and shining down into the middle of this snow globe is the statue in the middle, and that is the human being, and that statue inside carries the Holy Spirit. When that statue then acknowledges that Light of Christ that shines down, that guides them, that leads them each and every day, it opens them up to connect with the Holy Spirit. The Holy Spirit is ignited by the Light that shines directly down into that statue and lights the fire within. This is that burning desire that humans feel to do good. This is that burning feeling; this is that tear they drop when they have done good and they know they are good. When they experience emotions, when they experience human emotions, just as we have mentioned in the past; human emotions cause fog inside that snow globe.

Every time that statue experiences something negative or something they "believe" is bad, fog will be created. When one does so many things that they believe are bad but that God may

142

not see as bad, but the earth sees as bad, that fog thickens and thickens and thickens and thickens. The fog thickens so the light coming from above isn't as strong anymore. The Light becomes scattered. The Holy Spirit still burns within, the desire to connect with God to lead that physical being back to the arms of the loving creator. That Holy Spirit still burns with that desire, so when this human has the fog of human emotions like guilt, anger, and despair filling up their field, their snow globe, this is when depression sets in and this is when real human instinct will kick in. Humans without souls are not necessarily good, so to speak, as civilization today would call it. They are mammals. Humans are creatures of instinct, just like animals. They eat, they sleep, they kill, they protect themselves, and they mate. This is what humans do. So in order to fully understand and feel the Holy Spirit within, one needs to ask if their snow globe will be purified by the Light of Christ and have these emotions, the sadness, the despair, removed. As this statue sitting in the middle of the snow globe asks for help, this fog dissipates, is taken away and is enveloped with the Light of Christ.

Therefore, the Holy Spirit is reignited back within that statue. So the Light never goes out (extinguished). What happens is interference is caused by the fogging of guilt. Humans feel guilt. Guilt is the biggest killer among human beings. One may begin completely connected with the Light and the Holy Spirit. They may not be religious, but they are a child, they are innocent. The Light of Christ is flowing through them igniting their Holy Spirit and this is their childhood. As they begin to be hurt and told not to do that, or "you're not supposed to do this," guilt begins to build. This guilt begins to block the connection between the God and the Holy Spirit within each soul.

As this child grows, this child learns rules, and this child might do things that are wrong. This may be a very dogmatic, religion-ruled household that this child is born into, and soon they will build up massive amounts of guilt, therefore blocking them from their creator. Guilt causes one to look outward at another's guilty nature. It is human-nature; it is the ego's nature,

143

to not look at oneself for what one has done when one feels guilt. One will not look at the things they have done, they will look at what others have done so that the ego feels better. Does this take away the fog? No, it deepens it because inside, the Holy Spirit, the Holy Spirit inside them, knows they are pointing fingers at others for things that they have done. So this is the human condition that runs rampant throughout earth. This is the human condition of the ego, of the emotions. The more people that understand, the more souls that understand that each and every human being on this planet is their brother; that they are all one, the faster they will clear the fog from their arena, their snow globe, their life and each and every human being will become more and more connected not only to themselves above, their Christ self, the Holy Spirit, their Higher Self, but they will also all be connected as one because they will realize that up above they are all one.

We bring to you this information in hopes that the words will be spread throughout your society to help these human beings to clear the fog. Healers like your daughter, Marisa, help those people to clear the fog in their snow globes, so to speak. You, Joe, help people to clear that fog in the words that you preach. You are a minister. This is the archetype that you carry. You preach and you carry the words of Christ and through your doing this, by honoring us, we are proud. We thank you for this and tell you now that you will help many to clear the fog from their snow globe that they call their life, their energy or as your daughter and all of her coworkers in the healing field would call and the metaphysical world would call, the aura. Clearing these hardships, clearing these damages to the human aura will help society completely. And sometimes the knowledge and knowing that the religion that someone was brought up in, the household they were brought up in, and realizing and knowing that the words you speak that explain that, then maybe they weren't so bad, maybe these rules were man-made.

Maybe God loves them no matter what. Maybe their Higher Self planned it this way. Maybe it's not all their fault, maybe it's their human nature, it's their ego; it's their emotions. This is not to blame bad behavior on the ego or emotions, but for one to completely understand that in turning their life and their will over to their Higher Self or God, or the Christ within, aka the Holy Spirit, one can begin to see their life as not being a life that is happening "to" them but a life that is in the palms of their hands. They may create the life that they desire. Life is not happening to them.

As people begin to understand this information and they begin to see and know that there is a Light within them regardless of whom or what they believe in, as long as they can believe that there is something greater than themselves The Light above, guiding and leading them, whether it be Christ, their Higher Self, their Soul, or Angels or Guides, does not matter as long as they believe that there is a Light greater than them, above them, guiding them and they can turn their will in life over to that higher being and the Holy Spirit will be ignited within them. This does not just have to be done only within the Christian faith. This can be done in any way a human mind and ego wishes. The key here is turning the ego and the will of the emotions over to the Light. [And in my words: Every day!]

Conclusion

Amnesia is the means to an end. So you must be asking: why is God revealing this to us now? The reason is because God is advancing our earth. God feels it is time to stop allowing graduated spirits from Hell to occupy earth. This all started in and around November of 2011.

We all have the Light of Christ in us. It doesn't matter what religion we follow, we all come to earth with this Light. In the Heavens, God is Light, so is the Holy Spirit, and so is their Son. Their enemies are the darkness, the deceiver, the imposter. Marisa and I protect ourselves every day by asking to be surrounded by His Light and His Shield. We both believe that we derive that protection from Christ, who also was Jesus, the man.

Christ is not the same as the man, Jesus. Jesus was the perfect human manifestation of God, or Christ. God is everything, literally. God created all and is all. One of the manifestations of Himself that God created was "personality" and His perfect personality is Christ. Jesus is the human manifestation of the "consciousness" and "personality" of God, Christ, the Son. But Jesus the child, man, teacher, father to his siblings, loving son of Mary, and sacrifice to save our souls from darkness, was a human just like you and I.

Christ manifested Himself at least twice prior to his arrival as Jesus, once as Krishna and again as Melchizedek. The Hindu faith teaches that there are three aspects of God in Brahma, the Everything, Krishna the Embodiment of the Everything, and Vishnu, the Consciousness of the Everything. The Jewish and subsequent Muslim religions were born when Melchizedek visited Abraham in his tent.

Who we are is a piece of a structure. God created the Holy Spirit first, which is the permeating Light of Himself and knowledge of Himself. God next created His personality, which is Christ. Call Christ the second soul created together by the Father and the Holy Spirit (the mother side of God). Christ then created Oversouls[10] to manage the cosmos and create Souls to

146

occupy the physical planes, the universes that the Father creates. These Souls contain the consciousness of God and of Christ and contain the blood of Christ, which is the Holy Spirit. These are the Children of God and we—you and I—are Children of the Soul/the Holy Spirit. Out of the billions of Souls created by Christ, each individual Soul then creates a Soul Pod, a Soul Family, and Soul Groups of which we are all a part.

The typical Soul Pod of the Soul is made up of about 1,500 created spirits of the Soul. These individual 1,500 spirits are called Higher Selves, which I personally like to call Lord. They are perfect aspects of the Soul. But there is one caveat, and that is that every Soul, starting with Christ, has free will. The purpose of God, through Christ, through the Souls, and through the Higher Selves and their Spirits, is to grow, to learn, to become more, but doing it in the way each of these links thinks is best. You and I, as humans, are the creation of our Higher Self, who is really "you," and we are sort of like players on a team, each player using their own will to accomplish the same goal, and that is to not only find the light in himself, but to recognize it in their neighbor as well.

You/your Lord planned to come to live on earth as a human. You have done this many times, but each time you plan your life, you do so to learn lessons. Your predetermined lessons are to find a way to exist with other humans with their plans, too. The crux of the entire mystery of living is that we all have amnesia. Yes, amnesia. Not one person remembers planning their lives while in spirit in conjunction with the Soul and Christ. But we did. Not even Jesus. Not even Krishna. Jesus awoke from

---

[10] The Oversoul has only been touched on here. In another book the structure of the universe and its dimensions, along with further discussion of the soul will be explained. To be as simple as I can be, there is only a very small handful of Oversouls. These are direct creations of Christ created to run the universes. Since "universes" is plural, we will go into that much further the next time around. It is only important at this writing to understand that there is a lineage between me, the human being, and God; one that is filled with the blood of Christ and the knowledge and understanding of God, the Holy Spirit.

His amnesia when He was baptized by John and then began His ministry (see Matthew 4: 13-17).

Hindus plan their lives with the comfort of Krishna, who preceded them. Jews find solace in the "I Am" and in the man with no beginning or end, Melchizedek. Christians find their partner in Jesus, who died on the cross in order to save them. Buddhists find the Buddha, who gives them wisdom. Yes, there is religion in Heaven because each religion is still one aspect of God and the Souls He creates along with their Free Will. Each religion is a form of structure and the means of finding your way through the amnesia. When someone prays, they are asking their Soul, their Higher Self/Lord, their Oversoul, Christ, and God how to get through the struggles of the human existence caused by the duality of the combined levels of beings occupying the earth. We are wise to recognize those small subconscious murmurs that we hear sometimes that tell us that there is something else going on. Unfortunately we don't know if that is our Soul speaking to us or whether it is just our own mind and ego. We just don't remember. Sometimes we feel like strangers in a strange land and, in reality, we really are!

Jesus redacted the rules of the Old Testament and made our lesson in life one to respect every other human as a piece of the light; Love your neighbor as yourself, but have the wisdom to turn away from evil. The other is to find peace and know God. One way of finding peace is through the establishment of boundaries between yourself and those who are in contact with you. Something as simple as setting boundaries will bring you closer to peace and therefore to God. When we are at peace, our Light of Christ will shine. We will naturally do the things we must do to bring love to ourselves and project it toward others, despite all the secular trappings around us. That whispering in your subconscious is Christ communicating with your soul through the Higher Self/Lord, who is actually you without the amnesia trying to guide your human/earthly vessel through the darkness that surrounds you. You can call this vessel your human body, your human mind, or your ego coupled with a pre-existing soul/spirit living with amnesia and trying to cope with a crazy world still influenced by Lucifer and his spirit, Satan.

There is a big problem, though, with being a human. We come, again, with amnesia from whence we came, which is what we call Heaven. We can't adequately describe Heaven, but in a simple example, I can say that we humans can understand that they said the earth is the small box of crayons with eight colors and Heaven is the jumbo box with sixty-four colors. Earth is part of Heaven because the jumbo box still includes the eight colors found in the small box of crayons. All we really know is that after death almost everyone is at peace because after going home to Heaven, they remember who they really are and what they came to earth to accomplish. We say "almost" because there are exceptions. Some spirits get stuck between here and the Light. Finding and accepting the Light is how you find peace and all the perks that go along with it. That is what your Souls want. Satan doesn't want God's Light. Satan wants to deceive you into darkness and pull you away from the light. Either way, we are all God's children, genetically a direct link to the Father, to Christ, the creator of souls. It's up to each of us to figure that out in order to find His greatest favor. Satan doesn't want you to find the Light; therefore, he wages the battle for your spirit. They, both Christ and Lucifer, are ultimately vying for your soul.

Just like life, we are not all equal in the development of our Souls. We are all graduates, yes, but graduates of different levels of growth. We grow with and from our experiences. We grow up with success and grow down with failures. There are Souls that have rebelled against Christ and have decided that they know what's best for the growth of the soul. Lucifer was one of those Souls. His devotees, fallen angels and former humans, work diligently to find humans who don't know they are spirit and light, who through the everyday hassles of life let their lights dim, let depression and sadness in to take over and therefore open themselves up to the persuasions of these misdirected and evil ones who want nothing better than to thumb their noses at Christ.

149

When our Lord creates a new spirit, you and me, our Spirit comes to earth as an empty vessel. It knows that it is a cup of the water from the large tank we call God, but we all have free will. These new souls are targets for Lucifer and his fallen angels. Lucifer is also called the devil and Satan, per the Bible. The Koran and other religious texts also call him by his name, Lucifer. Lucifer chose to battle God for his created souls. The purpose of this battle is somewhat known, but may be impossible to fully understand. Lucifer wants to have everything his way. He just wants your soul and doesn't care about the means and consequences. He is a deceiver and a liar, but he is also a created soul by God that used to be, and probably still is, in charge of our earth.

Marisa and I believe that those who cannot accept the Light live in darkness. You and I have to deal with it in this crazy world of God's design. Earth, to you and me, is virtually the center of the universe, and to God it is a battle ground between Himself and the prince of darkness, Lucifer, better known as Satan. The entire universe is focused on earth. You would not believe the audience to your life. Nearly every created soul of God who called earth home at one time is watching the war between good and evil to see how this experiment turns out.

All that I can conclude from these conversations is that besides the battle taking place all around us, the way to the light along with peace in your life is to do exactly what Jesus said:

Love your neighbor as yourself and love God with all your heart and soul.

If everyone did that, good would win out over evil.

If you ask for God's blessings every morning when you wake up and then turn your will over to the Father, then the whole universe goes to work to keep you on your designed life plan of peace, love, and spiritual growth. For those we have been able to convey this message to, the first impulse or thought that comes to their minds is:

Are my guiding angels and passed loved ones with me when I go to the bathroom?

(That was my first thought also and the answer is no). Remember, they think of us as little, lost children. We also ask:

If we are graduated souls in Heaven and then do stupid things on earth, not necessarily evil things, will we be judged and possibly "demoted" by being stupid?

The way they described it to us is by example:

If you work in a successful company, then you likely have a much respected boss guiding you. This boss is an example of a good person living an upstanding life, and you admire him or her. Now you have a Christmas party, and your boss has a little too much egg nog and starts dancing and ends up dancing as awful as Elaine from the show *Seinfeld* (hopefully every one of you has seen that episode. It is absolutely hilarious). Of course you have a good natured laugh at your boss, but you also continue to respect him the next day at work when both of you have a chuckle about the party. We are all Elaines at one time or another. Our Lords/Higher Selves/Teachers/Guides just chuckle, too. They don't judge us for being stupid sometimes. And, in most cases, they've been human before themselves and they very much remember what it was like. It's true when they say "been there, done that!"

Epilogue

Our next book is slated to be about the mysteries regarding the structure of the soul as well as the structure of the universes and dimensions. But I'm fascinated by the mysteries of the earth. I'm also very interested in the secular world of politics. I have asked the other side if I can learn more through Marisa about things like dinosaurs, UFOs, the pyramids, the lost world of Atlantis, Stonehenge, crop circles, and other fascinating mysteries but they said we need to do what Jesus said:

A house built on sand will not stand and there must be a solid foundation of knowing God to grow on.

That foundation is the better explanation and understanding of the administration of God, and that is what we have tried to do here. Figuratively speaking, we have attempted to explain quantum physics to all us kindergarteners.

One of our next efforts will be to look at life's mysteries. We have been told that we now live in earth's third civilization. The first one wiped itself out through power and greed about one million years ago. They were universal travelers. Apparently, there were three different alien groups that tried to coexist on the earth, but it turned into failure and left the earth uninhabitable for almost 400,000 years. The second civilization was human souls evolved from the elements of the earth. This was eventually wiped out by the flood of Noah because of the same elements of power and greed that wiped out the first civilization. The flood is also when the continent of Atlantis was destroyed, along with all its comprehensive knowledge and understanding. So we are now in the third civilization, and we seem to be headed down that same road of destruction of power and greed. Lord, help us all!

I am eager to tape new conversations with the angels above and thus be able to expose the mysteries that scientists, astrologists, geologists, archeologists, and others have been trying forever to uncover in hopes that understanding our past will guide us to the peace that God wants us to ultimately find. That is going to be fun.

Stay tuned.

Joe Moris/Dad

Made in the USA
San Bernardino, CA
19 November 2013